ROBERT JHONSON

THE ROLE OF THE PSYCHOLOGIST IN CREATING WELL- BEING IN THE WORKPLACE

4H CAPITAL

In the dynamic landscape of today's corporate world, the heartbeat of any successful organization resonates not just in its bottom line, but in the intangible essence that defines its character—its corporate culture. Having dedicated over two decades to the intricate dance of strategies, support, and success across diverse sectors and companies, I have come to a resolute conclusion: the nucleus of prosperity lies within the creed of an organization.

This book, "The Psychologist's Role in Creating Workplace Wellbeing," is more than a guide; it is a voyage into the very soul of corporate culture. It unravels the tapestry of values, beliefs, and vision that, when acknowledged, articulated, and shared, become the guiding light steering organizations toward unparalleled success. As an experienced navigator of organizational psychology, I invite you to embark on a transformative journey—one that not only recognizes the profound impact of corporate culture on success but places the psychologist at the helm of identifying, shaping, and fortifying this cultural compass.

Within these pages, we will explore the profound influence of corporate culture on employee well-being, delving into the nuanced strategies that psychologists wield to mold and metamorphose it. From psychological interventions to leadership development, fostering psychological safety to enhancing emotional intelligence, this comprehensive guide offers practical insights and tools for psychologists and managers alike. The narrative extends beyond the confines of the workplace, emphasizing the crucial facets of work-life balance, conflict resolution, and robust employee support programs as vital components of holistic well-being.

In a world where change is constant, measurement and evaluation techniques become our compass, guiding psychologists in a continuous pursuit of improving workplace well-being and championing positive transformation. As we navigate this terrain together, let this book serve as a beacon—a testament to the indispensable role of the psychologist in shaping not just successful organizations but nurturing environments that thrive on the principles of well-being.

Join me in unraveling the intricate interplay of psychology and corporate culture—a journey that promises not only to enrich our understanding but to empower us to create workplaces that resonate with the harmony of success and well-being.

Robert Jhonson

CHAPTER I

UNDERSTANDING CORPORATE CULTURE

Corporate culture refers to the shared values, beliefs, attitudes, and behaviors that shape the work environment within an organization. It encompasses the norms, traditions, and practices that guide how employees interact with each other, as well as with clients, customers, and stakeholders. Corporate culture is often considered the "personality" of an organization, as it influences the overall atmosphere, employee engagement, and the organization's ability to achieve its goals.

A strong corporate culture is characterized by a clear mission and vision, a set of core values, and a positive work environment that fosters collaboration, innovation, and employee well-being. It is essential for organizations to define and cultivate a healthy corporate culture, as it directly impacts employee satisfaction, productivity, and overall organizational success.

1.1.1 The Elements of Corporate Culture

To understand corporate culture, it is important to identify its key elements. These elements shape the organization's values, behaviors, and practices, and contribute to the overall work environment. Some of the common elements of corporate culture include:

Core Values

Core values are the fundamental beliefs and principles that guide the actions and decisions of individuals within the organization. They serve as a compass for employees, helping them understand what is important and how they should behave. Core values can include integrity, respect, teamwork, innovation, and customer focus, among others. These values should be clearly defined and communicated to all employees to ensure alignment and consistency in behavior.

Communication

Effective communication is crucial for a healthy corporate culture. Open and transparent communication channels foster trust, collaboration, and engagement among employees. It allows for the free flow of information, ideas, and feedback, enabling employees to feel heard and valued. Clear communication also helps in aligning employees with the organization's goals and objectives, ensuring everyone is working towards a common purpose.

Leadership

Leadership plays a vital role in shaping corporate culture. The actions, behaviors, and decisions of leaders have a significant impact on the work environment and employee well-being. Effective leaders set the tone for the organization, embodying the desired values and behaviors. They inspire and motivate employees, provide guidance and support, and create a culture of trust and accountability.

Employee Engagement

Employee engagement refers to the level of commitment, passion, and enthusiasm employees have towards their work and the organization. A positive corporate culture promotes high levels of employee engagement, as it fosters a sense of belonging, purpose, and fulfillment. Engaged employees are more likely to be productive, innovative, and loyal to the organization.

Diversity and Inclusion

A diverse and inclusive corporate culture recognizes and values the unique perspectives, backgrounds, and experiences of all employees. It promotes equal opportunities, fairness, and respect for individuals, regardless of their gender, race, ethnicity, age, or other characteristics. Embracing diversity and inclusion enhances creativity, innovation, and problem-solving within the organization.

Work-Life Balance

A healthy corporate culture acknowledges the importance of work-life balance and supports employees in achieving it. It recognizes that employees have personal lives and commitments outside of work and encourages a flexible and supportive work environment. Promoting work-life balance helps reduce stress, improve well-being, and enhance employee satisfaction and retention.

1.1.2 The Role of the Psychologist in Defining Corporate Culture

Psychologists play a crucial role in understanding and shaping corporate culture. They bring their expertise in human behavior, motivation, and organizational dynamics to help organizations create a positive and aware culture. The psychologist's role in defining corporate culture includes:

Assessing Current Culture

Psychologists can conduct assessments and surveys to understand the existing corporate culture within an organization. They use various research methods and tools to gather data on employee perceptions, values, and behaviors. By analyzing this data, psychologists can identify strengths, weaknesses, and areas for improvement in the current culture.

Identifying Values and Behaviors

Psychologists work with organizational leaders and employees to identify the core values and desired behaviors that align with the organization's mission and vision. They facilitate discussions, workshops, and focus groups to gather input and consensus on the values that should guide the organization. This process ensures that the values are meaningful, relevant, and embraced by all stakeholders.

Developing Cultural Guidelines

Based on the identified values and behaviors, psychologists help develop cultural guidelines or a code of conduct that outlines the expected norms and behaviors within the organization. These guidelines serve as a reference for employees, providing clarity on how they should interact with each other and with external stakeholders. Psychologists ensure that the guidelines are communicated effectively and integrated into the organization's policies and practices.

Training and Development

Psychologists design and deliver training programs to educate employees about the desired culture and the behaviors that support it. These programs may include workshops on communication skills, teamwork, diversity and inclusion, and conflict resolution. By providing employees with the necessary knowledge and skills, psychologists empower them to contribute to a positive and aware corporate culture.

Change Management

When organizations undergo significant changes, such as mergers, acquisitions, or restructuring, psychologists play a vital role in managing the cultural transition. They help employees navigate the change process, address resistance, and adapt to the new culture. Psychologists provide support and guidance to leaders and employees, ensuring a smooth and successful cultural transformation.

In summary, the psychologist's role in defining corporate culture is to assess the current culture, identify values and behaviors, develop cultural guidelines, provide training and development, and support change management. By leveraging their expertise in human behavior and organizational dynamics, psychologists contribute to creating a positive, aware, and healthy corporate culture that promotes employee well-being and organizational success.

1.2 The Importance of Corporate Culture

Corporate culture plays a vital role in shaping the overall well-being and success of an organization. It encompasses the shared values, beliefs, attitudes, and behaviors that define the work environment and guide the actions of employees. A positive corporate culture fosters employee engagement, productivity, and satisfaction, while a toxic culture can lead to stress, burnout, and low morale. Recognizing the significance of corporate culture, psychologists have a crucial role to play in creating and maintaining a healthy and aware culture within the workplace.

The impact of corporate culture on the well-being of employees cannot be overstated. A positive culture promotes a sense of belonging, trust, and psychological safety, which are essential for employee engagement and motivation. When employees feel valued, supported, and respected, they are more likely to be satisfied with their work, experience lower levels of stress, and have a higher overall well-being.

On the other hand, a toxic corporate culture can have detrimental effects on employees' mental and emotional health. It can lead to increased levels of stress, anxiety, and even depression. In such environments, employees may feel unsupported, undervalued, and constantly under pressure to meet unrealistic expectations. This can result in decreased job satisfaction, higher turnover rates, and a decline in overall productivity.

Psychologists play a crucial role in understanding and shaping corporate culture to create a positive and aware work environment. They bring their expertise in human behavior, motivation, and organizational psychology to assess, analyze, and intervene in the culture of an organization. By working closely with leaders, managers, and employees, psychologists can help identify areas of improvement and develop strategies to enhance the overall well-being of the workforce.

One of the primary responsibilities of psychologists in shaping corporate culture is to assess the existing culture and identify its strengths and weaknesses. Through surveys, interviews, and observations, they gather data to understand the values, norms, and behaviors that define the organization. This assessment helps in identifying any toxic elements within the culture and determining the necessary steps for improvement.

Psychologists also play a vital role in creating awareness and educating leaders and employees about the importance of corporate culture. They help individuals understand how their actions and behaviors contribute to the overall culture of the organization. By promoting open communication and providing training on topics such as diversity and inclusion, conflict resolution, and stress management, psychologists empower employees to actively participate in creating a positive work environment.

Once the existing culture has been assessed, psychologists collaborate with organizational leaders to develop strategies for cultural change. This involves setting clear goals and objectives for the desired culture and identifying the necessary steps to achieve them. Psychologists help leaders understand the importance of aligning the culture with the organization's values and goals, as well as the potential benefits of a positive culture on employee well-being and organizational performance.

Psychologists also assist in developing policies and practices that support the desired culture. This may involve revising performance evaluation systems, implementing flexible work arrangements, or promoting work-life balance initiatives. By integrating well-being programs and practices into the fabric of the organization, psychologists help create a culture that prioritizes the mental, emotional, and physical health of employees.

Implementing cultural change requires a systematic approach and ongoing commitment from all levels of the organization. Psychologists work closely with leaders and managers to ensure that the desired changes are effectively communicated and implemented. They provide guidance on how to engage employees in the change process, address resistance, and create a sense of ownership and accountability.

Psychologists also play a crucial role in sustaining cultural change over time. They help organizations monitor progress, evaluate the effectiveness of interventions, and make necessary adjustments. By regularly assessing the culture and gathering feedback from employees, psychologists ensure that the desired changes are embedded in the organization's DNA and continue to support employee well-being and organizational success.

In conclusion, corporate culture has a significant impact on the well-being of employees and the overall success of an organization. Psychologists play a vital role in understanding, shaping, and maintaining a positive and aware culture within the workplace. By assessing the existing culture, developing strategies for change, and implementing sustainable interventions, psychologists contribute to creating a work environment that promotes employee well-being, engagement, and productivity.

1.3 The Role of the Psychologist in Understanding Corporate Culture

Understanding corporate culture is crucial for creating a positive and healthy work environment. This is where the role of a psychologist becomes essential. Psychologists have the expertise to analyze and interpret the various aspects of corporate culture, enabling them to provide valuable insights and guidance for creating an aware and supportive culture.

Analyzing Organizational Values and Beliefs

One of the primary responsibilities of a psychologist in understanding corporate culture is to analyze the organization's values and beliefs. These values and beliefs serve as the foundation upon which the entire culture is built. By conducting interviews, surveys, and focus groups, psychologists can gather data to identify the core values and beliefs that drive the organization. This information helps in understanding the underlying principles that guide employee behavior and decision-making processes.

Psychologists can also assess the alignment between the stated values and the actual practices within the organization. This analysis helps identify any discrepancies or inconsistencies that may exist, allowing for targeted interventions to bridge the gap between the desired and actual culture.

Assessing Organizational Norms and Behaviors

In addition to values and beliefs, psychologists also play a crucial role in assessing the norms and behaviors prevalent within the organization. Norms are the unwritten rules and expectations that govern employee behavior, while behaviors refer to the actions and interactions observed in the workplace. By observing and analyzing these norms and behaviors, psychologists can gain insights into the prevailing culture and its impact on employee well-being.

Psychologists can conduct surveys, focus groups, and observations to assess the norms and behaviors within the organization. They can identify patterns of behavior that may contribute to a positive or negative work environment. This assessment helps in understanding the cultural dynamics and identifying areas for improvement.

Another important role of the psychologist in understanding corporate culture is to identify the strengths and weaknesses of the existing culture. By conducting comprehensive assessments, psychologists can determine the aspects of the culture that contribute positively to employee well-being and those that may hinder it.

Psychologists can use various assessment tools, such as cultural audits and employee satisfaction surveys, to gather data on different dimensions of the culture. This information helps in identifying the cultural strengths that can be leveraged to enhance well-being and the weaknesses that need to be addressed.

Providing Recommendations for Cultural Improvement

Based on their analysis and assessment of the corporate culture, psychologists can provide valuable recommendations for cultural improvement. These recommendations are aimed at creating a more aware and supportive culture that promotes employee well-being.

Psychologists can suggest interventions and strategies to align the culture with the desired values and beliefs. They can propose initiatives to enhance communication, collaboration, and employee engagement. Additionally, psychologists can provide guidance on fostering a culture of psychological safety, where employees feel comfortable expressing their opinions and concerns without fear of negative consequences.

Facilitating Cultural Change

Implementing cultural change within an organization can be a complex and challenging process. Psychologists play a crucial role in facilitating this change by providing support and guidance to leaders and employees. They can help develop change management strategies, create awareness about the need for cultural change, and provide training and development programs to support the transition.

Psychologists can also assist in monitoring and evaluating the progress of cultural change initiatives. By collecting and analyzing data, they can assess the effectiveness of interventions and make necessary adjustments to ensure sustained improvement.

Collaborating with Leadership and HR

To effectively understand and shape corporate culture, psychologists need to collaborate closely with leadership and human resources (HR) departments. They can work together to develop strategies, policies, and programs that align with the desired culture and promote employee well-being.

Psychologists can provide training and development programs for leaders to enhance their understanding of the impact of culture on employee well-being. They can also collaborate with HR to integrate cultural assessments and interventions into the employee lifecycle, from recruitment and onboarding to performance management and career development.

In conclusion, the role of the psychologist in understand-ding corporate culture is crucial for creating a positive and healthy work environment. By analyzing values, beliefs, norms, and behaviors, psychologists can identify cultural strengths and weaknesses and provide recommendations for improvement. They play a vital role in facilitating cultural change and collaborating with leadership and HR to create an aware and supportive culture that enhances employee well-being.

1.4 Methods for Assessing Corporate Culture

Assessing corporate culture is a crucial step in understanding the dynamics and values that shape an organization. By evaluating the existing culture, psychologists can identify areas of strength and areas that require improvement. This assessment provides valuable insights into the organization's values, beliefs, and behaviors, allowing psychologists to develop strategies for creating a positive and healthy work environment. In this section, we will explore some of the methods psychologists use to assess corporate culture.

Surveys and Questionnaires

One of the most common methods for assessing corporate culture is through the use of surveys and questionnaires. These tools allow psychologists to gather information directly from employees, providing valuable insights into their perceptions and experiences within the organization. Surveys can be designed to measure various aspects of corporate culture, such as communication, teamwork, leadership, and employee well-being.

Psychologists can create customized surveys tailored to the specific needs of the organization. These surveys typically include a combination of closed-ended and open-ended questions to gather both quantitative and qualitative data. Closed-ended questions provide respondents with predefined response options, allowing for easy analysis and comparison. Open-ended questions, on the other hand, encourage employees to provide detailed feedback and insights into their experiences.

By analyzing the survey responses, psychologists can identify patterns and trends within the organization. They can determine the level of employee satisfaction, identify areas of concern, and assess the alignment between the stated values and the actual behaviors within the organization. This information serves as a foundation for developing strategies to improve corporate culture and enhance employee well-being.

In addition to surveys, psychologists often conduct interviews and focus groups to gain a deeper understanding of corporate culture. These qualitative methods allow for more in-depth exploration of employees' experiences, perceptions, and attitudes. By engaging in direct conversations, psychologists can uncover valuable insights that may not be captured through surveys alone.

Interviews involve one-on-one discussions between psychologists and employees. These conversations provide an opportunity for employees to share their thoughts, concerns, and suggestions in a confidential setting. Psychologists can ask probing questions to delve deeper into specific aspects of corporate culture and gain a comprehensive understanding of the organization's dynamics.

Focus groups, on the other hand, involve a small group of employees who come together to discuss specific topics related to corporate culture. These group discussions encourage participants to share their perspectives, engage in dialogue, and build upon each other's ideas. Focus groups provide a collaborative environment where employees can express their opinions and contribute to the assessment of corporate culture.

Both interviews and focus groups allow psychologists to gather rich qualitative data that complements the quantitative data obtained through surveys. These methods provide a more holistic understanding of corporate culture by capturing the nuances, complexities, and underlying dynamics that shape the organization.

Observations and Ethnographic Research

Another method psychologists use to assess corporate culture is through observations and ethnographic research. By immersing themselves in the organization's environment, psychologists can directly observe the behaviors, interactions, and norms that define the corporate culture.

Observations involve psychologists actively observing employees' behaviors, communication patterns, and interactions within the workplace. This method allows psychologists to gain firsthand insights into the organization's culture and identify any discrepancies between the stated values and the actual behaviors exhibited by employees.

Ethnographic research takes observation a step further by involving psychologists in the daily activities of the organization. This method allows psychologists to experience the organization's culture from an insider's perspective, gaining a deeper understanding of the values, rituals, and social dynamics that shape the workplace.

Through observations and ethnographic research, psychologists can identify both explicit and implicit aspects of corporate culture. They can uncover unwritten rules, power dynamics, and informal communication channels that influence employee well-being and organizational performance. This method provides a comprehensive view of the organization's culture and helps psychologists develop targeted interventions to create a positive and healthy work environment.

Document Analysis

Psychologists also rely on document analysis as a method for assessing corporate culture. This involves reviewing various organizational documents, such as mission statements, vision statements, employee handbooks, and company policies. By analyzing these documents, psychologists can gain insights into the organization's stated values, goals, and expectations.

Document analysis allows psychologists to assess the alignment between the organization's stated values and the actual practices within the workplace. It helps identify any discrepancies or gaps that may exist between the organization's espoused culture and its enacted culture. By understanding these gaps, psychologists can develop strategies to bridge them and create a more congruent and authentic corporate culture.

In addition to formal documents, psychologists may also analyze informal communication channels, such as internal memos, emails, and social media platforms. These sources provide valuable insights into the organization's communication patterns, employee interactions, and the overall climate within the workplace.

By combining multiple methods of assessment, psychologists can develop a comprehensive understanding of corporate culture. This holistic approach allows them to identify strengths, weaknesses, and areas for improvement within the organization. Armed with this knowledge, psychologists can then develop targeted interventions to create a positive and healthy work environment that promotes employee well-being and organizational success.

CHAPTER II

THE IMPACT OF CORPORATE CULTURE ON EMPLOYEE WELL-BEING

The relationship between corporate culture and employee well-being is complex and multifaceted, with culture having a profound impact on various aspects of employees' lives, including their mental health, job satisfaction, and overall quality of life.

Corporate culture has a direct influence on employee well-being. A positive and supportive culture fosters a sense of belonging, trust, and psychological safety among employees. It promotes open communication, collaboration, and teamwork, which are essential for creating a healthy work environment. In contrast, a toxic or negative culture can have detrimental effects on employees' mental and emotional well-being, leading to increased stress, burnout, and decreased job satisfaction.

A positive corporate culture promotes employee well-being by providing a supportive and inclusive work environment. It values work-life balance, encourages personal growth and development, and recognizes and rewards employees' contributions. Such a culture fosters a sense of purpose and meaning in employees' work, enhancing their overall job satisfaction and engagement.

A toxic corporate culture can have a detrimental impact on employee well-being and overall organizational success. As a psychologist, it is crucial to be able to identify the signs of a toxic corporate culture in order to address and rectify the issues that may be present. By recognizing these signs, psychologists can play a vital role in creating a healthier and more positive work environment.

Lack of Open Communication

One of the key signs of a toxic corporate culture is a lack of open communication within the organization. In such an environment, employees may feel hesitant to express their opinions, concerns, or ideas. This can lead to a lack of collaboration, innovation, and trust among team members.

As a psychologist, it is important to observe the communication patterns within the organization and identify any barriers that may be hindering open and honest dialogue.

High Turnover Rates

Another sign of a toxic corporate culture is high turnover rates. When employees are dissatisfied with their work environment, they are more likely to seek opportunities elsewhere. A toxic culture may contribute to feelings of burnout, stress, and a lack of job satisfaction. As a psychologist, it is essential to monitor turnover rates and identify any underlying issues that may be causing employees to leave the organization.

Lack of Trust and Transparency

A toxic corporate culture often lacks trust and transparency. Employees may feel that their contributions are undervalued, and decisions are made without their input. This can lead to a sense of disengagement and a lack of commitment to the organization's goals. Psychologists can identify signs of mistrust and work with leadership to foster a culture of transparency and open communication.

Micromanagement and Lack of Autonomy

Micromanagement is a common characteristic of a toxic corporate culture. When employees are constantly monitored and have limited autonomy, it can lead to feelings of frustration, demotivation, and a lack of job satisfaction. Psychologists can identify signs of micromanagement and work with leaders to promote a more empowering and autonomous work environment.

High Levels of Stress and Burnout

A toxic corporate culture often contributes to high levels of stress and burnout among employees. Excessive workloads, unrealistic expectations, and a lack of work-life balance can take a toll on employees' mental and physical well-being. Psychologists can assess the levels of stress and burnout within the organization and develop strategies to promote well-being and resilience.

Lack of Diversity and Inclusion

A toxic corporate culture may also be characterized by a lack of diversity and inclusion. When employees do not feel valued or included, it can lead to feelings of isolation, discrimination, and a lack of psychological safety. Psychologists can assess the organization's diversity and inclusion practices and work with leadership to create a more inclusive and equitable work environment.

Resistance to Change

In a toxic corporate culture, there is often resistance to change and a lack of adaptability. This can hinder innovation, growth, and the ability to respond to market demands. Psychologists can identify signs of resistance to change and work with leaders to foster a culture of continuous improvement and learning.

Lack of Work-Life Balance

A toxic corporate culture may prioritize work over employees' personal lives, leading to a lack of work-life balance. This can result in increased stress, burnout, and decreased productivity. Psychologists can assess the organization's policies and practices related to work-life balance and develop strategies to promote a healthier integration of work and personal life.

Bullying and Harassment

A toxic corporate culture may also be characterized by bullying and harassment. When employees are subjected to mistreatment, it can have severe psychological and emotional consequences. Psychologists can identify signs of bullying and harassment and work with leadership to implement policies and procedures that promote a safe and respectful work environment.

Lack of Employee Development and Growth Opportunities

In a toxic corporate culture, there may be a lack of emphasis on employee development and growth opportunities. This can lead to feelings of stagnation, disengagement, and a lack of motivation. Psychologists can assess the organization's practices related to employee development and work with leaders to create a culture that values continuous learning and professional growth.

By identifying these signs of a toxic corporate culture, psychologists can play a crucial role in creating awareness and initiating positive change within organizations. Through their expertise in understanding human behavior and organizational dynamics, psychologists can help create a healthier and more supportive work environment that promotes employee well-being and organizational success.

2.2 The Psychological Effects of a Negative Corporate Culture

A negative corporate culture can have profound psychological effects on employees, impacting their well-being and overall mental health. When employees are subjected to a toxic work environment, it can lead to a range of negative emotions, stress, and even physical health issues. In this section, we will explore the psychological effects of a negative corporate culture and the importance of addressing these issues for the well-being of employees.

Increased Stress and Anxiety

One of the most significant psychological effects of a negative corporate culture is increased stress and anxiety among employees. In a toxic work environment, employees may constantly feel pressured, undervalued, and unsupported. This constant stress can lead to a variety of physical and mental health problems, including high blood pressure, insomnia, depression, and burnout.

Employees who experience chronic stress and anxiety are more likely to have difficulty concentrating, making decisions, and managing their emotions. This can result in decreased productivity, increased absenteeism, and a higher turnover rate. It is crucial for organizations to recognize the impact of a negative corporate culture on employee well-being and take steps to address and mitigate these effects.

Decreased Job Satisfaction and Motivation

A negative corporate culture can also significantly impact employees' job satisfaction and motivation. When employees are subjected to a toxic work environment, they may feel unappreciated, disengaged, and demotivated. This can lead to a decrease in productivity and a lack of commitment to the organization.

Employees who are dissatisfied with their work environment are more likely to experience feelings of frustration, resentment, and apathy. They may become disinterested in their work, leading to a decline in the quality of their output. Additionally, a negative corporate culture can erode employees' trust in their leaders and colleagues, further exacerbating job dissatisfaction and reducing motivation.

Negative Impact on Mental Health

A negative corporate culture can have a detrimental effect on employees' mental health. Constant exposure to a toxic work environment can contribute to the development or exacerbation of mental health conditions such as anxiety disorders, depression, and even post-traumatic stress disorder (PTSD).

Employees who experience a negative corporate culture may feel isolated, unsupported, and emotionally drained.

This can lead to feelings of hopelessness, helplessness, and a loss of self-esteem. The stigma surrounding mental health in the workplace may also prevent employees from seeking the necessary support and treatment, further worsening their mental well-being.

Strained Interpersonal Relationships

A toxic work environment can strain interpersonal relationships among employees. When a negative corporate culture promotes competition, backstabbing, and a lack of trust, it can create a hostile and divisive atmosphere. Employees may feel compelled to protect themselves at the expense of their colleagues, leading to strained relationships and a breakdown in teamwork.

The psychological effects of strained interpersonal relationships can be significant. Employees may experience feelings of loneliness, isolation, and a lack of belonging. This can further contribute to stress, anxiety, and a decline in overall well-being. It is essential for organizations to foster a positive and supportive work environment that encourages collaboration, open communication, and trust among employees.

Impact on Work-Life Balance

A negative corporate culture can also have a detrimental effect on employees' work-life balance. When a toxic work environment demands long hours, promotes a culture of presenteeism, and fails to prioritize the well-being of employees, it can lead to an imbalance between work and personal life.

Employees who struggle to maintain a healthy work-life balance may experience increased stress, fatigue, and a lack of fulfillment outside of work. This imbalance can negatively impact their relationships, physical health, and overall quality of life. Organizations must recognize the importance of promoting work-life balance and create policies and practices that support employees in achieving this balance.

In conclusion, a negative corporate culture can have severe psychological effects on employees. Increased stress and anxiety, decreased job satisfaction and motivation, negative impacts on mental health, strained interpersonal relationships, and an imbalance between work and personal life are all consequences of a toxic work environment. It is crucial for organizations to prioritize the well-being of their employees and take proactive measures to address and rectify a negative corporate culture. By doing so, they can create a healthier and more productive work environment for everyone involved.

2.3 Promoting Well-being in a Positive Corporate Culture

Creating a positive corporate culture is essential for promoting employee well-being in the workplace. A positive corporate culture fosters a supportive and inclusive environment where employees feel valued, motivated, and engaged. In this section, we will explore the role of the psychologist in promoting well-being in a positive corporate culture.

Understanding the Role of the Psychologist

Psychologists play a crucial role in understanding and promoting well-being in the workplace. They have the expertise to assess the psychological climate within an organization and identify areas that may be impacting employee well-being. By understanding the unique dynamics of the organization, the psychologist can develop strategies to promote a positive corporate culture.

Psychologists can collaborate with organizational leaders and HR professionals to create awareness about the importance of well-being in the workplace. They can educate employees and management about the benefits of a positive corporate culture and the impact it has on individual and organizational performance. By highlighting the connection between well-being and productivity, psychologists can help organizations prioritize employee well-being as a strategic goal.

Creating a Supportive Work Environment

One of the key roles of the psychologist in promoting well-being in a positive corporate culture is to create a supportive work environment. This involves fostering a culture of respect, empathy, and open communication. Psychologists can work with leaders to develop policies and practices that promote work-life balance, flexibility, and employee autonomy.

Psychologists can also help organizations implement employee support programs, such as employee assistance programs (EAPs) and mental health initiatives. These programs provide employees with resources and support to address personal and work-related challenges, ultimately enhancing their well-being. By collaborating with HR professionals, psychologists can ensure that these programs are accessible, confidential, and tailored to the specific needs of the organization.

Promoting Positive Relationships and Collaboration

Positive relationships and collaboration are essential for a healthy corporate culture. Psychologists can facilitate team-building activities and workshops that promote positive communication, trust, and collaboration among employees. By fostering a sense of belonging and camaraderie, psychologists can help create a supportive and cohesive work environment.

Psychologists can also provide conflict resolution training to employees and managers. By equipping individuals with effective conflict resolution skills, psychologists can help prevent and address conflicts in a constructive manner. This promotes a positive corporate culture where differences are respected, and conflicts are resolved in a fair and respectful manner.

Encouraging Employee Growth and Development

A positive corporate culture values employee growth and development. Psychologists can work with organizational leaders to create opportunities for professional development, skill-building, and career advancement. By providing employees with the resources and support they need to grow, psychologists can enhance their sense of fulfillment and well-being in the workplace.

Psychologists can also assist in the implementation of performance management systems that focus on employee strengths and development. By shifting the focus from a purely evaluative approach to a developmental one, psychologists can help create a culture that values continuous learning and improvement. This not only enhances employee well-being but also contributes to the overall success of the organization.

Promoting Work-Life Balance

Work-life balance is crucial for employee well-being. Psychologists can collaborate with organizational leaders to develop policies and practices that promote work-life balance. This may include flexible work arrangements, remote work options, and the promotion of self-care practices.

Psychologists can also educate employees and managers about the importance of setting boundaries between work and personal life. By promoting healthy work habits and encouraging employees to prioritize self-care, psychologists can help create a positive corporate culture that supports work-life balance.

Evaluating and Improving Well-being Initiatives

Continuous evaluation and improvement are essential for maintaining a positive corporate culture and promoting employee well-being. Psychologists can assist organizations in measuring and assessing the effectiveness of well-being initiatives. By collecting and analyzing data, psychologists can identify areas of improvement and make evidence-based recommendations for enhancing well-being in the workplace.

Psychologists can also collaborate with HR professionals to develop strategies for sustaining well-being initiatives in the long term. By monitoring progress, adapting interventions, and addressing emerging challenges, psychologists can ensure that the positive corporate culture and well-being initiatives remain a priority within the organization.

In conclusion, the role of the psychologist in promoting well-being in a positive corporate culture is multifaceted. Psychologists can create awareness about the importance of well-being, foster a supportive work environment, promote positive relationships and collaboration, encourage employee growth and development, promote work-life balance, and evaluate and improve well-being initiatives. By working collaboratively with organizational leaders and HR professionals, psychologists can contribute to the creation of a positive corporate culture that enhances employee well-being and organizational success.

CHAPTER III

THE ROLE OF THE PSYCHOLOGIST IN SHAPING CORPORATE CULTURE

Corporate culture plays a significant role in the overall well-being and success of an organization. It encompasses the shared values, beliefs, attitudes, and behaviors that define the work environment and shape employee experiences. A positive corporate culture fosters employee engagement, productivity, and satisfaction, while a toxic culture can lead to stress, burnout, and low morale. As such, the role of the psychologist in shaping corporate culture is crucial in creating a healthy and supportive work environment.

The psychologist plays a vital role in shaping corporate culture by understanding, assessing, and influencing the various factors that contribute to the work environment. They bring their expertise in human behavior, motivation, and organizational dynamics to create a culture that supports employee well-being and organizational success.

The psychologist acts as a change agent within the organization, advocating for the importance of a positive culture and driving the necessary changes. They work closely with leaders, managers, and employees to create awareness, build consensus, and overcome resistance to change. The psychologist helps individuals and teams understand the benefits of a healthy culture and empowers them to contribute to its development.

Creating a positive corporate culture requires collaboration with various stakeholders, including HR professionals, managers, and employees. The psychologist works closely with these stakeholders to align their efforts and ensure a coordinated approach to cultural change. They provide training, coaching, and support to managers and employees to help them understand their role in shaping the culture.

The psychologist plays a crucial role in evaluating and monitoring the effectiveness of cultural change initiatives. They use various assessment tools and metrics to measure the impact of the interventions and identify areas for improvement. By regularly evaluating the progress, the psychologist can make necessary adjustments and ensure that the desired culture is being cultivated.

3.2 Creating a Vision for a Positive Corporate Culture

Creating a positive corporate culture is essential for the well-being and success of an organization. It sets the tone for how employees interact with each other, how they approach their work, and ultimately, how they feel about their jobs. As a psychologist, your role in shaping corporate culture is crucial. You have the expertise to understand the psychological dynamics at play within an organization and can help create a vision for a positive corporate culture.

Understanding the Importance of Corporate Culture

Before diving into creating a vision for a positive corporate culture, it is important to understand why corporate culture matters. Corporate culture encompasses the shared values, beliefs, and behaviors that define an organization. It influences employee attitudes, motivation, and overall well-being. A positive corporate culture fosters a sense of belonging, encourages collaboration, and promotes employee engagement. On the other hand, a toxic culture can lead to stress, burnout, and low morale.

Assessing the Current Corporate Culture

To create a vision for a positive corporate culture, it is crucial to assess the current state of the organization's culture. This assessment helps identify areas that need improvement and provides a baseline for measuring progress. As a psychologist, you can employ various methods to assess corporate culture, such as surveys, interviews, and focus groups. These tools allow you to gather insights from employees at all levels of the organization and gain a comprehensive understanding of the existing culture.

During the assessment process, it is important to consider both the formal and informal aspects of corporate culture. Formal aspects include policies, procedures, and organizational structure, while informal aspects encompass the unwritten rules, norms, and values that guide employee behavior. By examining both formal and informal elements, you can gain a holistic view of the organization's culture and identify areas for improvement.

Defining the Desired Culture

Once you have assessed the current corporate culture, the next step is to define the desired culture. This involves creating a vision for the organization that aligns with its values, goals, and mission. As a psychologist, you can facilitate this process by engaging with key stakeholders, including senior leaders, managers, and employees. By involving a diverse range of perspectives, you can ensure that the desired culture reflects the needs and aspirations of the entire organization.

When defining the desired culture, it is important to consider the organization's unique context and industry. What works for one organization may not work for another. Additionally, the desired culture should be aligned with the organization's strategic objectives and support its long-term success. For example, if innovation is a key goal, the desired culture may emphasize creativity, risk-taking, and open communication.

Communicating the Vision

Once the desired culture has been defined, it is crucial to effectively communicate the vision to all employees. Clear and consistent communication is essential for creating buy-in and ensuring that everyone understands the direction the organization is heading. As a psychologist, you can assist in developing communication strategies that effectively convey the vision and its importance.

Communication should be ongoing and involve various channels, such as town hall meetings, newsletters, and intranet platforms. It is important to provide opportunities for employees to ask questions, share their thoughts, and provide feedback. By fostering open and transparent communication, you can create a sense of ownership and involvement among employees, increasing their commitment to the desired culture.

Aligning Policies and Practices

Creating a vision for a positive corporate culture is not enough; it must be supported by policies and practices that align with the desired culture. As a psychologist, you can work with organizational leaders and HR professionals to review and revise existing policies and practices to ensure they are in line with the desired culture.

For example, if the desired culture emphasizes work-life balance, policies may need to be revised to include flexible work arrangements, wellness programs, and supportive leave policies. By aligning policies and practices with the desired culture, you create a consistent and supportive environment that reinforces the values and behaviors necessary for a positive culture.

Leading by Example

As a psychologist, you have a unique opportunity to lead by example and model the desired culture. Your actions and behaviors can inspire others and create a ripple effect throughout the organization. By demonstrating the values and behaviors associated with the desired culture, you can influence others to do the same.

Leading by example involves consistently practicing what you preach, treating others with respect, and fostering a supportive and inclusive environment. It also means being open to feedback and continuously learning and growing. By embodying the desired culture, you can inspire others to do the same and create a positive and thriving work environment.

Monitoring and Adjusting

Creating a vision for a positive corporate culture is an ongoing process. It requires continuous monitoring and adjustment to ensure that the desired culture is being effectively implemented and maintained. As a psychologist, you can assist in developing metrics and evaluation methods to measure the progress of cultural change initiatives.

Regular feedback from employees, surveys, and performance indicators can provide valuable insights into the effectiveness of the cultural change efforts. Based on this feedback, adjustments can be made to policies, practices, and communication strategies to address any gaps or challenges. By continuously monitoring and adjusting, you can ensure that the organization remains on track towards achieving the desired culture.

In conclusion, as a psychologist, your role in creating a vision for a positive corporate culture is vital. By understanding the importance of corporate culture, assessing the current culture, defining the desired culture, communicating the vision, aligning policies and practices, leading by example, and monitoring and adjusting, you can help shape a culture that promotes well-being and success in the workplace.

3.3 Developing Strategies for Cultural Change

Creating a positive and healthy corporate culture is essential for the well-being and success of employees and the organization as a whole. As a psychologist, your role in shaping corporate culture is crucial. In this section, we will explore the strategies you can employ to facilitate cultural change within an organization.

Before embarking on any cultural change initiative, it is important to assess the current culture of the organization. This assessment will help you understand the strengths and weaknesses of the existing culture and identify areas that require improvement. You can use various methods such as surveys, interviews, and focus groups to gather information about employees' perceptions of the culture.

During the assessment process, it is important to create a safe and confidential environment where employees feel comfortable sharing their thoughts and experiences. This will enable you to gain valuable insights into the underlying dynamics of the culture and identify any toxic or negative elements that may be impacting employee well-being.

Defining the Desired Culture

Once you have assessed the current culture, the next step is to define the desired culture. This involves creating a vision for the future state of the organization and identifying the values, behaviors, and norms that will contribute to a positive and healthy culture.

To define the desired culture, you can engage in collaborative discussions with key stakeholders, including senior leaders, managers, and employees. This will help ensure that the vision is aligned with the organization's goals and values and that it resonates with the employees.

As a psychologist, you can facilitate these discussions by using your expertise in organizational psychology and your understanding of human behavior. You can help the organization articulate its values and translate them into specific behaviors that can be practiced and reinforced within the workplace.

Once the desired culture has been defined, the next step is to create a comprehensive change plan. This plan should outline the strategies and actions that will be taken to shift the culture towards the desired state.

The change plan should include specific goals, timelines, and responsibilities. It should also identify the resources and support needed to implement the plan effectively. As a psychologist, you can play a key role in developing this plan by providing insights into the psychological and behavioral aspects of cultural change.

When creating the change plan, it is important to consider the unique characteristics of the organization and its employees. Different organizations may require different approaches to cultural change, and it is important to tailor the strategies to fit the specific context.

Engaging and Empowering Employees

Employee engagement and empowerment are critical for successful cultural change. As a psychologist, you can help create strategies to engage and empower employees throughout the change process.

One strategy is to involve employees in decision-making and problem-solving. This can be done through focus groups, workshops, and team meetings where employees have the opportunity to contribute their ideas and perspectives. By involving employees in the change process, you can increase their sense of ownership and commitment to the new culture.

Another strategy is to provide training and development opportunities that support the desired culture. This can include workshops on communication skills, conflict resolution, and emotional intelligence. By equipping employees with the necessary skills and knowledge, you can empower them to contribute to a positive and healthy culture.

Communicating and Reinforcing the Change

Effective communication is essential for successful cultural change. As a psychologist, you can help develop a communication plan that ensures the change message is effectively delivered to all employees.

The communication plan should include regular updates, town hall meetings, and other channels to keep employees informed about the progress of the cultural change initiative. It should also provide opportunities for employees to ask questions, share their concerns, and provide feedback.

In addition to communication, it is important to reinforce the change through consistent actions and behaviors. This can be done through recognition and rewards systems that align with the desired culture. By recognizing and rewarding employees who demonstrate the desired behaviors, you can reinforce the cultural change and motivate others to follow suit.

Monitoring and Evaluating Progress

Monitoring and evaluating the progress of cultural change is essential to ensure its effectiveness and sustainability. As a psychologist, you can help develop metrics and evaluation methods to assess the impact of the cultural change initiative.

Regular surveys, focus groups, and performance evaluations can be used to gather feedback from employees and measure their perceptions of the culture. This feedback can then be used to make adjustments to the change plan and address any challenges or barriers that may arise.

By monitoring and evaluating progress, you can identify areas of success and areas that require further attention.

This continuous improvement approach will help ensure that the cultural change initiative remains on track and that the desired culture is achieved and maintained.

In conclusion, as a psychologist, your role in shaping corporate culture is vital. By assessing the current culture, defining the desired culture, creating a change plan, engaging and empowering employees, communicating and reinforcing the change, and monitoring and evaluating progress, you can help facilitate cultural change within an organization. Through your expertise in psychology and understanding of human behavior, you can contribute to the creation of a positive and healthy corporate culture that promotes employee well-being and organizational success.

CHAPTER IV

PSYCHOLOGICAL INTERVENTIONS FOR ENHANCING WELL-BEING IN THE WORKPLACE

Workplace stress is a common issue that can have a significant impact on employee well-being and productivity. As a psychologist, it is crucial to identify and understand the various stressors that exist within the workplace. By recognizing these stressors, psychologists can develop effective strategies to mitigate their negative effects and create a healthier work environment.

Workplace stress refers to the physical, emotional, and psychological strain experienced by individuals in response to work-related demands and pressures. It can arise from various sources, including excessive workload, time pressure, lack of control, interpersonal conflicts, and organizational changes.

4.1.1 Common Workplace Stressors

To effectively address workplace stress, psychologists must be able to identify the common stressors that employees may encounter. While the specific stressors can vary depending on the industry and organizational context, there are several common stressors that are frequently observed in the workplace:

Excessive Workload

One of the most prevalent stressors is an excessive workload. When employees are faced with an overwhelming number of tasks and responsibilities, they may experience high levels of stress and struggle to meet deadlines. This can lead to feelings of burnout, decreased job satisfaction, and reduced productivity.

Lack of Control

A lack of control over one's work environment can also contribute to workplace stress. When employees feel that they have little say in decision-making processes or are unable to influence their work conditions, they may experience a sense of powerlessness and frustration. This lack of control can lead to increased stress levels and a decrease in overall well-being.

Interpersonal Conflicts

Interpersonal conflicts among colleagues or with supervisors can significantly impact employee well-being. When individuals experience conflict in the workplace, it can create a hostile and tense environment, leading to increased stress levels. Resolving these conflicts and promoting positive relationships is essential for creating a healthy work environment.

Organizational Changes

Organizational changes, such as mergers, restructurings, or downsizings, can be highly stressful for employees. These changes often bring uncertainty, job insecurity, and increased work demands. The fear of potential job loss or changes in roles and responsibilities can lead to heightened stress levels and decreased job satisfaction.

Work-Life Imbalance

Achieving a healthy work-life balance is a challenge for many employees. When individuals feel overwhelmed by work demands and struggle to find time for personal activities and relationships, it can lead to increased stress levels and a decline in overall well-being. Addressing work-life imbalance is crucial for promoting employee well-being and reducing workplace stress.

4.1.2 Assessing Workplace Stressors

To effectively address workplace stress, psychologists must employ various assessment methods to identify and understand the specific stressors present in an organization. These assessment methods can include:

Surveys and questionnaires can be valuable tools for gathering information about workplace stressors. By asking employees to provide feedback on their work environment, workload, relationships, and other relevant factors, psychologists can gain insights into the specific stressors that individuals are experiencing.

Interviews and Focus Groups

Conducting interviews and focus groups allows psychologists to engage in more in-depth discussions with employees. These qualitative methods provide an opportunity to explore individual experiences, perceptions, and concerns related to workplace stress. By listening to employees' stories and perspectives, psychologists can gain a deeper understanding of the stressors that exist within the organization.

Observation and Work Analysis

Psychologists can also observe employees in their work environment to identify potential stressors. By observing work processes, interactions, and behaviors, psychologists can identify areas of concern and potential sources of stress. Work analysis can provide valuable insights into the specific tasks, demands, and pressures that employees face on a daily basis.

4.1.3 The Psychologist's Role in Addressing Workplace Stressors

Once workplace stressors have been identified, psychologists play a crucial role in developing strategies to address and mitigate their impact. Some key roles that psychologists can undertake include:

Psychologists can offer individual support to employees who are experiencing high levels of stress. Through counseling and therapy sessions, psychologists can help individuals develop coping mechanisms, manage stress, and improve their overall well-being. By addressing individual stressors, psychologists can contribute to creating a healthier work environment.

Implementing Stress Management Programs

Psychologists can design and implement stress management programs within organizations. These programs can include workshops, training sessions, and educational materials that provide employees with the necessary tools and techniques to manage stress effectively. By equipping employees with stress management skills, psychologists can help reduce the negative impact of workplace stress.

Collaborating with Management and HR

Psychologists can collaborate with management and human resources departments to develop policies and practices that promote a healthy work environment. By advocating for changes in workload distribution, work-life balance initiatives, and conflict resolution strategies, psychologists can contribute to creating a culture that prioritizes employee well-being.

Conducting Organizational Interventions

Psychologists can also conduct organizational interventions to address workplace stressors. These interventions may involve restructuring work processes, improving communication channels, and implementing policies that support employee well-being. By addressing the root causes of workplace stress, psychologists can create lasting changes that benefit both individuals and the organization as a whole.

In conclusion, identifying workplace stressors is a crucial step in creating a healthier work environment. Psychologists play a vital role in recognizing and understanding these stressors, allowing them to develop effective strategies to address and mitigate their impact. By providing individual support, implementing stress management programs, collaborating with management, and conducting organizational interventions, psychologists can contribute to creating a workplace that promotes employee well-being and productivity.

4.2 Stress Management Techniques

Stress is an inevitable part of the modern workplace. It can arise from various sources such as heavy workloads, tight deadlines, interpersonal conflicts, and organizational changes. If left unaddressed, chronic stress can have detrimental effects on employees' well-being, productivity, and overall job satisfaction. As a psychologist, it is crucial to understand and implement effective stress management techniques to promote a healthy and productive work environment.

4.2.1 Promoting Work-Life Balance

One effective stress management technique is promoting work-life balance. Many employees struggle to find a balance between their work responsibilities and personal life, leading to increased stress levels. Psychologists can work with organizations to implement policies and practices that support work-life balance, such as flexible work schedules, remote work options, and encouraging employees to take regular breaks.

Additionally, psychologists can provide education and training on time management and prioritization skills. By helping employees manage their time effectively, psychologists can reduce stress levels and improve overall well-being.

4.2.2 Providing Stress Reduction Techniques

Psychologists can also teach employees various stress reduction techniques to help them cope with workplace stress. These techniques can include relaxation exercises, deep breathing exercises, mindfulness meditation, and guided imagery. By incorporating these techniques into their daily routines, employees can better manage stress and improve their overall well-being.

Psychologists can conduct workshops or training sessions to teach employees these stress reduction techniques. They can also provide resources such as online videos or mobile applications that employees can access at their convenience. By equipping employees with these tools, psychologists empower them to take an active role in managing their stress levels.

4.2.3 Encouraging Physical Activity

Regular physical activity has been shown to be an effective stress management technique. Exercise releases endorphins, which are natural mood boosters, and helps reduce stress hormones in the body. Psychologists can encourage employees to incorporate physical activity into their daily routines by promoting workplace wellness programs, organizing group exercise sessions, or providing access to fitness facilities.

Psychologists can also educate employees about the benefits of physical activity and provide resources on how to incorporate exercise into their busy schedules. By promoting physical activity, psychologists not only help employees manage stress but also improve their overall health and well-being.

4.2.4 Implementing Stress Reduction Programs

In addition to individual stress management techniques, psychologists can also implement stress reduction programs within organizations. These programs can include stress management workshops, support groups, and counseling services. By providing employees with a safe space to discuss their stressors and learn coping strategies, psychologists can help create a supportive work environment.

Psychologists can also collaborate with human resources departments to develop policies and procedures that promote a stress-free workplace. This can include implementing flexible work arrangements, establishing clear communication channels, and providing resources for employees to seek help when needed.

4.2.5 Encouraging Self-Care

Self-care is an essential aspect of stress management. Psychologists can educate employees about the importance of self-care and provide guidance on how to incorporate self-care practices into their daily lives. This can include encouraging employees to take regular breaks, practice self-reflection, engage in hobbies or activities they enjoy, and seek social support.

By promoting self-care, psychologists help employees prioritize their well-being and create a healthier work-life balance. This, in turn, reduces stress levels and improves overall job satisfaction.

4.2.6 Creating a Supportive Work Environment

Psychologists play a crucial role in creating a supportive work environment that fosters stress management. They can work with organizational leaders to develop policies and practices that prioritize employee well-being. This can include promoting open communication, encouraging feedback, and providing resources for employees to seek help when needed.

Psychologists can also train managers and supervisors on how to recognize and address signs of stress in their team members. By equipping leaders with the skills to support their employees, psychologists contribute to a positive work environment where stress is effectively managed.

In conclusion, the role of the psychologist in stress management is vital for creating a healthy and productive work environment. By identifying sources of stress, promoting work-life balance, providing stress reduction techniques, encouraging physical activity, implementing stress reduction programs, encouraging self-care, and creating a supportive work environment, psychologists can help employees effectively manage stress and improve their overall well-being.

4.3 Building Resilience in Employees

Resilience is a crucial factor in promoting well-being in the workplace. It refers to an individual's ability to bounce back from adversity, adapt to change, and maintain a positive mindset in the face of challenges. Building resilience in employees is essential for creating a healthy and productive work environment. Psychologists play a vital role in helping organizations develop strategies to enhance resilience among their employees.

4.3.1 Understanding Resilience

Before delving into the strategies for building resilience, it is important to understand what resilience entails. Resilience is not about being immune to stress or avoiding difficult situations; rather, it is about developing the skills and mindset to effectively cope with and recover from adversity. Resilient individuals are better equipped to handle stress, maintain a positive outlook, and adapt to change. They are more likely to bounce back from setbacks and continue performing at their best.

4.3.2 Identifying Factors that Impact Resilience

To effectively build resilience in employees, it is crucial to identify the factors that can either enhance or hinder resilience. Some of the key factors that impact resilience include:

4.3.2.1 Supportive Work Environment

A supportive work environment is essential for fostering resilience. When employees feel valued, supported, and encouraged, they are more likely to develop resilience. This can be achieved through open communication, positive feedback, and providing resources for personal and professional growth.

4.3.2.2 Work-Life Balance

Maintaining a healthy work-life balance is crucial for building resilience. When employees have time for self-care, relaxation, and pursuing personal interests, they are better equipped to handle stress and challenges in the workplace. Organizations can promote work-life balance by implementing flexible work arrangements, encouraging time off, and promoting a culture that values personal well-being.

4.3.2.3 Training and Development Opportunities

Providing employees with opportunities for growth and development is another important factor in building resilience. When individuals have the necessary skills and knowledge to handle their responsibilities effectively, they feel more confident and capable of overcoming challenges. Organizations can offer training programs, mentorship opportunities, and continuous learning initiatives to enhance employee resilience.

4.3.2.4 Social Support

Having a strong support system is crucial for building resilience. Organizations can foster social support by encouraging teamwork, collaboration, and creating opportunities for employees to connect and build relationships. Peer support programs, team-building activities, and employee resource groups can all contribute to a supportive social environment.

4.3.3 Strategies for Building Resilience

Psychologists can work closely with organizations to develop strategies for building resilience in employees. Here are some effective strategies that psychologists can implement:

4.3.3.1 Promoting Self-Awareness

Self-awareness is a fundamental aspect of resilience. Psychologists can help employees develop self-awareness by encouraging reflection, mindfulness practices, and self-assessment tools. By understanding their strengths, weaknesses, and triggers, employees can better manage their emotions and responses to challenging situations.

4.3.3.2 Providing Stress Management Techniques

Psychologists can teach employees effective stress management techniques to help them cope with workplace pressures. These techniques may include deep breathing exercises, mindfulness meditation, time management strategies, and relaxation techniques. By equipping employees with these tools, psychologists empower them to better handle stress and maintain their well-being.

4.3.3.3 Building Emotional Intelligence

Emotional intelligence is a key component of resilience. Psychologists can help employees develop emotional intelligence by providing training on self-awareness, empathy, and effective communication. By understanding and managing their emotions, employees can navigate difficult situations more effectively and build stronger relationships with colleagues.

4.3.3.4 Encouraging Growth Mindset

Psychologists can promote a growth mindset among employees, which is the belief that abilities and intelligence can be developed through effort and learning. By encouraging employees to embrace challenges, learn from failures, and persist in the face of setbacks, psychologists can foster a resilient mindset.

4.3.3.5 Providing Supportive Resources

Psychologists can collaborate with organizations to provide supportive resources for employees. This may include access to counseling services, employee assistance programs, and wellness initiatives. By offering these resources, organizations demonstrate their commitment to employee well-being and provide a safety net for employees during challenging times.

4.3.4 Sustaining Resilience

Building resilience is an ongoing process that requires continuous effort and support. Psychologists can assist organizations in sustaining resilience by:

4.3.4.1 Regular Training and Development

Organizations should provide regular training and development opportunities to reinforce resilience-building skills. This can include workshops, seminars, and online resources that focus on stress management, emotional intelligence, and other relevant topics.

4.3.4.2 Creating a Supportive Culture

Organizations should foster a culture that values resilience and well-being. This can be achieved by recognizing and rewarding resilient behaviors, promoting work-life balance, and encouraging open communication. When resilience is embedded in the organizational culture, employees are more likely to embrace and sustain it.

Psychologists can help organizations monitor and evaluate the effectiveness of resilience-building initiatives. By collecting feedback, conducting surveys, and analyzing data, organizations can identify areas for improvement and make necessary adjustments to their strategies.

4.3.4.4 Leadership Support

Leadership plays a crucial role in sustaining resilience. Psychologists can work with leaders to ensure they model resilient behaviors, provide support to their teams, and create an environment that encourages resilience. When leaders prioritize and support resilience, it becomes ingrained in the organizational culture.

Building resilience in employees is a collaborative effort that requires the expertise of psychologists and the commitment of organizations. By implementing effective strategies and providing ongoing support, organizations can create a resilient workforce that thrives in the face of challenges and contributes to a positive and productive work environment.

CHAPTER V

THE ROLE OF LEADERSHIP IN CREATING A HEALTHY WORK ENVIRONMENT

5.1 The Impact of Leadership on Employee Well-being

Leadership plays a crucial role in shaping the well-being of employees within an organization. Effective leadership can create a positive work environment that fosters employee engagement, satisfaction, and overall well-being. On the other hand, poor leadership can contribute to a toxic work culture, leading to increased stress, burnout, and decreased productivity. In this section, we will explore the impact of leadership on employee well-being and discuss strategies for developing effective leadership styles.

5.1.1 The Importance of Leadership in Employee Well-being

Leadership sets the tone for the entire organization. The way leaders interact with their employees, make decisions, and communicate expectations greatly influences the well-being of the workforce. When leaders prioritize employee well-being, it creates a culture of support, trust, and respect. Employees feel valued and motivated, leading to increased job satisfaction and productivity.

On the other hand, when leaders neglect employee well-being, it can have detrimental effects on the workforce. Lack of support, micromanagement, and a focus solely on results can lead to high levels of stress, dissatisfaction, and even mental health issues among employees. It is essential for leaders to recognize the impact they have on their employees' well-being and take proactive steps to create a healthy work environment.

5.1.2 Developing Effective Leadership Styles

Effective leadership styles are those that prioritize the well-being of employees while also driving organizational success. Here are some key characteristics of effective leadership styles:

5.1.2.1 Empathy and Emotional Intelligence

Leaders who demonstrate empathy and emotional intelligence are better equipped to understand and respond to the needs of their employees. They are able to build strong relationships, provide support, and create a sense of belonging within the organization. By recognizing and validating the emotions of their employees, leaders can foster a positive work environment that promotes well-being.

5.1.2.2 Clear Communication

Effective leaders communicate openly and transparently with their employees. They provide clear expectations, feedback, and guidance, which helps employees feel informed and engaged. Regular communication also allows leaders to address any concerns or issues promptly, preventing them from escalating and negatively impacting employee well-being.

5.1.2.3 Trust and Empowerment

Leaders who trust their employees and empower them to make decisions and take ownership of their work create a sense of autonomy and job satisfaction. When employees feel trusted and empowered, they are more likely to be motivated, innovative, and committed to their work. This, in turn, positively impacts their well-being.

5.1.2.4 Support and Recognition

Effective leaders provide support and recognition to their employees. They offer guidance, resources, and opportunities for growth and development. Recognizing and appreciating employees' efforts and achievements boosts morale and enhances their sense of well-being. It is important for leaders to create a culture of appreciation and celebrate the successes of their team members.

5.1.3 Building Trust and Communication within the Organization

Building trust and effective communication within an organization is essential for promoting employee well-being. Here are some strategies for leaders to foster trust and communication:

5.1.3.1 Lead by Example

Leaders must lead by example and demonstrate the behaviors they expect from their employees. By modeling open communication, active listening, and respect, leaders can create a culture where employees feel comfortable expressing their thoughts and concerns.

5.1.3.2 Encourage Feedback and Collaboration

Leaders should actively encourage feedback from their employees and create opportunities for collaboration. This can be done through regular team meetings, one-on-one discussions, and anonymous feedback channels. By involving employees in decision-making processes and valuing their input, leaders can foster a sense of ownership and engagement.

5.1.3.3 Provide Training and Development

Leaders should invest in training and development programs that enhance communication and interpersonal skills. This can include workshops on active listening, conflict resolution, and emotional intelligence. By equipping leaders with the necessary skills, they can effectively communicate with their teams and address any conflicts or issues that may arise.

5.1.3.4 Foster a Supportive Environment

Leaders should create a supportive environment where employees feel comfortable seeking help and support. This can be achieved by implementing employee assistance programs, providing resources for mental health support, and promoting work-life balance. By prioritizing employee well-being, leaders can create a culture that values the holistic health of their workforce.

5.1.4 Empowering Employees for Success

Empowering employees is a crucial aspect of leadership that contributes to their well-being. Here are some strategies for leaders to empower their employees:

5.1.4.1 Delegate Responsibility

Leaders should delegate tasks and responsibilities to their employees, allowing them to take ownership of their work. By giving employees autonomy and trust, leaders empower them to make decisions and contribute to the success of the organization. This sense of empowerment enhances employee well-being and job satisfaction.

5.1.4.2 Provide Growth Opportunities

Leaders should provide opportunities for growth and development to their employees. This can include training programs, mentorship, and career advancement opportunities. By investing in the professional growth of their employees, leaders demonstrate their commitment to their well-being and create a motivated and engaged workforce.

5.1.4.3 Recognize and Reward Achievements

Leaders should recognize and reward the achievements of their employees. This can be done through verbal praise, public recognition, or tangible rewards. By acknowledging their employees' efforts and contributions, leaders boost morale and create a positive work environment that fosters well-being.

Leaders should encourage creativity and innovation within their teams. By providing a safe space for employees to share their ideas and take calculated risks, leaders empower them to contribute to the growth and success of the organization. This sense of empowerment and involvement positively impacts employee well-being.

In conclusion, leadership has a significant impact on employee well-being. Effective leaders prioritize employee well-being, develop strong communication and trust within the organization, and empower their employees for success. By adopting these strategies, leaders can create a positive work environment that promotes the well-being and overall success of their employees.

5.2 Developing Effective Leadership Styles

Leadership plays a crucial role in creating a healthy work environment and promoting employee well-being. Effective leadership styles can have a significant impact on the overall corporate culture and the well-being of employees. In this section, we will explore the role of the psychologist in developing effective leadership styles that foster a positive and supportive work environment.

5.2.1 Understanding Leadership Styles

Leadership styles refer to the approach and behavior of leaders in influencing and guiding their teams. Different leadership styles can have varying effects on employee well-being and the overall corporate culture. It is essential for leaders to understand their own leadership style and its impact on their team members.

There are several leadership styles commonly observed in organizations, including:

1. **Autocratic Leadership**: In this style, leaders make decisions without consulting their team members.

They have complete control and authority over the decision-making process.

2. **Democratic Leadership**: This style involves leaders who actively involve their team members in the decision-making process. They encourage participation, collaboration, and open communication.

3. **Transformational Leadership**: Transformational leaders inspire and motivate their team members to achieve their full potential. They focus on individual growth, development, and empowerment.

4. **Laissez-Faire Leadership**: Leaders with this style provide minimal guidance and supervision to their team members. They allow employees to make decisions and take responsibility for their work.

5. **Servant Leadership**: Servant leaders prioritize the needs of their team members and focus on supporting and serving them. They promote a culture of empathy, collaboration, and personal development.

5.2.2 The Role of the Psychologist in Developing Effective Leadership Styles

Psychologists play a vital role in helping leaders develop effective leadership styles that promote employee well-being and create a positive corporate culture. They provide valuable insights and guidance based on their understanding of human behavior, motivation, and organizational dynamics.

Psychologists can assist leaders in the following ways:

1. Assessing Leadership Styles

Psychologists can assess the existing leadership styles within an organization to identify their strengths and weaknesses. Through various assessment tools and techniques, they can provide leaders with a comprehensive understanding of their leadership style's impact on employee well-being and organizational culture.

2. Providing Feedback and Coaching

Psychologists can provide leaders with constructive feedback and coaching to enhance their leadership skills. They can help leaders identify areas for improvement and develop strategies to address them. By working closely with leaders, psychologists can support their personal and professional growth, enabling them to become more effective in their roles.

3. Developing Emotional Intelligence

Emotional intelligence is a critical aspect of effective leadership. Psychologists can help leaders develop their emotional intelligence skills, including self-awareness, self-regulation, empathy, and social skills. By enhancing emotional intelligence, leaders can better understand and connect with their team members, fostering a positive and supportive work environment.

4. Facilitating Leadership Development Programs

Psychologists can design and facilitate leadership development programs tailored to the specific needs of leaders and the organization. These programs can include workshops, training sessions, and coaching sessions to enhance leadership skills, promote self-reflection, and encourage continuous learning and growth.

5. Promoting Ethical Leadership

Ethical leadership is essential for creating a healthy work environment and maintaining employee well-being. Psychologists can educate leaders about ethical principles and help them integrate these principles into their leadership practices. By promoting ethical decision-making and behavior, leaders can build trust, credibility, and respect within their teams.

5.2.3 The Benefits of Effective Leadership Styles

Developing effective leadership styles has numerous benefits for both employees and organizations. When leaders adopt leadership styles that prioritize employee well-being and create a positive work environment, the following outcomes can be observed:

1. Increased Employee Engagement

Effective leadership styles promote employee engagement by fostering a sense of purpose, autonomy, and mastery. Engaged employees are more committed, motivated, and productive, leading to improved organizational performance.

2. Enhanced Job Satisfaction

Leaders who prioritize employee well-being and create a supportive work environment contribute to higher levels of job satisfaction among their team members. Satisfied employees are more likely to be loyal, dedicated, and proactive in their roles.

3. Reduced Stress and Burnout

Leadership styles that promote work-life balance, open communication, and support can help reduce stress and prevent burnout among employees. When employees feel supported and valued, they are less likely to experience excessive stress and exhaustion.

4. Improved Collaboration and Teamwork

Effective leadership styles encourage collaboration, teamwork, and open communication within teams. When leaders create an environment where diverse perspectives are valued and encouraged, employees are more likely to work together harmoniously and achieve collective goals.

Employees who work under effective leaders are more likely to stay with the organization for the long term. When leaders prioritize employee well-being and create a positive work environment, employees feel valued and are less likely to seek opportunities elsewhere.

In conclusion, the role of the psychologist in developing effective leadership styles is crucial for creating a healthy work environment and promoting employee well-being. By assessing leadership styles, providing feedback and coaching, developing emotional intelligence, facilitating leadership development programs, and promoting ethical leadership, psychologists can help leaders become more effective in their roles. The benefits of effective leadership styles include increased employee engagement, enhanced job satisfaction, reduced stress and burnout, improved collaboration and teamwork, and higher retention rates.

5.3 Building Trust and Communication within the Organization

Building trust and effective communication within an organization is crucial for creating a healthy and productive work environment. Trust and open communication foster collaboration, innovation, and employee well-being. As a psychologist, you play a vital role in facilitating the development of trust and effective communication within the organization. This section will explore the strategies and techniques you can employ to build trust and enhance communication among employees.

5.3.1 The Importance of Trust in the Workplace

Trust is the foundation of any successful organization. When employees trust their leaders and colleagues, they feel safe, valued, and supported. Trust creates a positive work environment where individuals can freely express their ideas, take risks, and collaborate effectively. It also promotes employee engagement, job satisfaction, and overall well-being. As a psychologist, you can help cultivate trust within the organization by implementing the following strategies:

5.3.1.1 Lead by Example

Leadership plays a crucial role in establishing trust within the organization. As a psychologist, you can work closely with leaders to help them understand the importance of leading by example. Encourage leaders to demonstrate trustworthiness, integrity, and transparency in their actions and decisions. When employees see their leaders acting with honesty and fairness, it sets a positive example and encourages trust among the workforce.

5.3.1.2 Foster Psychological Safety

Psychological safety is the belief that one can speak up, share ideas, and take risks without fear of negative consequences. It is a fundamental aspect of building trust and effective communication within the organization. As a psychologist, you can help create a psychologically safe environment by promoting open dialogue, active listening, and non-judgmental attitudes. Encourage leaders to create spaces where employees feel comfortable expressing their thoughts and concerns without fear of retribution.

5.3.1.3 Establish Clear Communication Channels

Effective communication is essential for building trust within the organization. As a psychologist, you can assist in establishing clear communication channels that facilitate open and transparent communication. Encourage leaders to implement regular team meetings, town halls, and feedback sessions to ensure that information flows freely and everyone has a voice. Additionally, promote the use of technology platforms that enable easy and efficient communication among employees.

5.3.2 Enhancing Communication Skills

Effective communication is a two-way process that involves both speaking and listening. As a psychologist, you can help employees and leaders enhance their communication skills to foster better understanding and collaboration. Here are some strategies you can employ:

5.3.2.1 Active Listening

Active listening is a crucial skill that promotes understanding and empathy. Encourage employees and leaders to practice active listening by giving their full attention, maintaining eye contact, and providing verbal and non-verbal cues to show understanding. Active listening helps build rapport, trust, and stronger relationships within the organization.

5.3.2.2 Nonviolent Communication

Nonviolent communication is a communication style that focuses on expressing needs and feelings without blaming or criticizing others. As a psychologist, you can teach employees and leaders the principles of nonviolent communication, such as using "I" statements, expressing empathy, and seeking mutual understanding. Nonviolent communication reduces conflicts, promotes understanding, and enhances trust within the organization.

5.3.2.3 Conflict Resolution Skills

Conflicts are inevitable in any workplace, but how they are resolved can either strengthen or weaken trust within the organization. As a psychologist, you can provide training and support in conflict resolution skills. Teach employees and leaders effective techniques for managing conflicts, such as active listening, finding common ground, and seeking win-win solutions. By resolving conflicts in a constructive manner, trust and communication can be preserved and even strengthened.

5.3.3 Promoting Collaboration and Teamwork

Collaboration and teamwork are essential for building trust and effective communication within the organization. As a psychologist, you can facilitate the development of collaborative work environments by implementing the following strategies:

5.3.3.1 Encouraging Cross-Functional Collaboration

Encourage employees from different departments or teams to collaborate on projects and initiatives. Cross-functional collaboration promotes knowledge sharing, diversity of ideas, and a sense of unity within the organization. As a psychologist, you can help create opportunities for cross-functional collaboration through team-building activities, workshops, and shared projects.

5.3.3.2 Team-Building Exercises

Team-building exercises can help foster trust, communication, and collaboration among team members. As a psychologist, you can design and facilitate team-building activities that encourage employees to work together, solve problems, and build stronger relationships. These exercises can range from outdoor activities to problem-solving games and workshops.

5.3.3.3 Recognition and Appreciation

Recognizing and appreciating the contributions of employees is essential for building trust and fostering teamwork. As a psychologist, you can work with leaders to implement recognition programs that celebrate individual and team achievements. Encourage leaders to provide regular feedback, acknowledge accomplishments, and create a culture of appreciation within the organization.

5.3.4 Overcoming Barriers to Trust and Communication

Despite efforts to build trust and enhance communication, organizations may face various barriers that hinder these processes. As a psychologist, you can help identify and overcome these barriers by:

5.3.4.1 Addressing Power Dynamics

Power dynamics within the organization can create barriers to trust and effective communication. As a psychologist, you can facilitate discussions and workshops that address power imbalances and promote equality and inclusivity. Encourage leaders to create a culture that values diverse perspectives and encourages open dialogue at all levels of the organization.

5.3.4.2 Managing Conflict

Unresolved conflicts can erode trust and hinder communication within the organization. As a psychologist, you can provide mediation and facilitation services to help resolve conflicts in a fair and constructive manner. By addressing conflicts promptly and effectively, you can prevent them from escalating and damaging relationships within the organization.

5.3.4.3 Promoting Cultural Sensitivity

Cultural differences can sometimes create barriers to trust and effective communication. As a psychologist, you can promote cultural sensitivity and awareness within the organization. Encourage employees and leaders to embrace diversity, respect different perspectives, and engage in cross-cultural communication training. By fostering a culturally inclusive environment, trust and communication can thrive.

In conclusion, as a psychologist, your role in building trust and effective communication within the organization is crucial. By promoting trust, enhancing communication skills, and fostering collaboration, you can create a work environment that supports employee well-being and organizational success.

5.4 Empowering Employees for Success

Empowering employees is a crucial aspect of creating a healthy and successful work environment. When employees feel empowered, they are more engaged, motivated, and productive. As a psychologist, your role in empowering employees is vital in fostering a culture of success within the organization. By providing support, guidance, and resources, you can help employees develop the skills and mindset necessary to thrive in their roles. This section will explore the various ways psychologists can empower employees for success.

5.4.1 Building Self-Efficacy

Self-efficacy refers to an individual's belief in their ability to succeed in specific tasks or situations. As a psychologist, you can play a significant role in building self-efficacy among employees. By providing them with opportunities to develop new skills, offering constructive feedback, and recognizing their achievements, you can help employees build confidence in their abilities. Encouraging employees to set realistic goals and providing them with the necessary support and resources to achieve those goals can also contribute to building self-efficacy.

5.4.2 Encouraging Autonomy

Empowering employees involves giving them a sense of autonomy and control over their work. As a psychologist, you can help create a work environment that encourages autonomy by promoting decision-making authority, allowing employees to have a say in their work processes, and providing opportunities for them to take on new responsibilities. By trusting employees to make decisions and giving them the freedom to explore innovative ideas, you can foster a sense of ownership and empowerment.

5.4.3 Providing Continuous Learning Opportunities

Continuous learning is essential for employee growth and development. As a psychologist, you can facilitate continuous learning by promoting a culture of learning within the organization. This can be achieved by organizing training programs, workshops, and seminars that enhance employees' skills and knowledge. Additionally, you can encourage employees to pursue further education or certifications relevant to their roles. By providing access to learning resources and supporting employees' professional development, you empower them to expand their capabilities and reach their full potential.

5.4.4 Promoting Collaboration and Teamwork

Collaboration and teamwork are crucial for success in any organization. As a psychologist, you can promote collaboration by fostering a culture of open communication, trust, and respect. Encourage employees to share ideas, collaborate on projects, and work together towards common goals. By facilitating team-building activities, promoting effective communication strategies, and resolving conflicts constructively, you can empower employees to work collaboratively and achieve collective success.

5.4.5 Recognizing and Rewarding Achievements

Recognition and rewards play a significant role in empowering employees. As a psychologist, you can advocate for a recognition program within the organization that acknowledges and rewards employees' achievements. This can be in the form of verbal praise, certificates, bonuses, or other incentives. By recognizing employees' efforts and contributions, you not only boost their morale but also reinforce a culture of success and empowerment.

5.4.6 Providing Emotional Support

Empowering employees goes beyond providing them with skills and resources; it also involves providing emotional support. As a psychologist, you can offer a safe and supportive space for employees to express their concerns, fears, and challenges. By actively listening, providing empathy, and offering guidance, you can help employees navigate through difficult situations and build resilience. By addressing their emotional well-being, you contribute to their overall success and empowerment.

5.4.7 Encouraging Work-Life Balance

Work-life balance is essential for employee well-being and success. As a psychologist, you can advocate for work-life balance within the organization by promoting flexible work arrangements, encouraging employees to take breaks and vacations, and setting boundaries between work and personal life. By emphasizing the importance of self-care and promoting a healthy work-life balance, you empower employees to prioritize their well-being, leading to increased productivity and success.

5.4.8 Providing Mentorship and Coaching

Mentorship and coaching programs can be powerful tools for empowering employees. As a psychologist, you can facilitate mentorship programs where experienced employees can guide and support their less-experienced colleagues. Additionally, you can provide coaching to employees, helping them set goals, develop action plans, and overcome challenges. By offering mentorship and coaching, you empower employees to learn from others' experiences, gain valuable insights, and grow both personally and professionally.

In conclusion, the role of the psychologist in empowering employees for success is crucial in creating a healthy and thriving work environment. By building self-efficacy, encouraging autonomy, providing continuous learning opportunities, promoting collaboration, recognizing achievements, offering emotional support, encouraging work-life balance, and providing mentorship and coaching, psychologists can empower employees to reach their full potential and contribute to the overall success of the organization.

CHAPTER VI

PROMOTING PSYCHOLOGICAL SAFETY IN THE WORKPLACE

6.1 Understanding Psychological Safety

Psychological safety is a crucial aspect of creating a healthy and productive work environment. It refers to the belief that one can express their thoughts, ideas, and concerns without fear of negative consequences such as ridicule, punishment, or rejection. When employees feel psychologically safe, they are more likely to take risks, share innovative ideas, and engage in open and honest communication. As a psychologist, understanding and promoting psychological safety within the workplace is an essential part of creating an aware corporate culture.

6.1.1 The Importance of Psychological Safety

Psychological safety is vital for fostering a positive work environment where employees feel comfortable and supported. When individuals feel safe to express themselves, they are more likely to contribute their unique perspectives and talents, leading to increased creativity, collaboration, and problem-solving. Moreover, psychological safety is closely linked to employee well-being, job satisfaction, and overall organizational performance.

In a psychologically safe workplace, employees are more likely to:

1. Speak up: When individuals feel safe, they are more willing to voice their opinions, concerns, and suggestions. This open communication allows for the identification and resolution of issues before they escalate.

2. Take risks: Psychological safety encourages employees to take calculated risks and explore new ideas without fear of failure or retribution. This fosters innovation and continuous improvement within the organization.

3. Learn and grow: When employees feel safe, they are more likely to seek feedback, ask questions, and engage in professional development opportunities. This promotes a culture of continuous learning and personal growth.

4. Collaborate effectively: Psychological safety enhances teamwork and collaboration by creating an environment where individuals trust and respect one another. This leads to better problem-solving, decision-making, and overall team performance.

6.1.2 Creating Psychological Safety

As a psychologist, you play a crucial role in creating and promoting psychological safety within the workplace. Here are some strategies to help foster a safe and supportive work environment:

6.1.2.1 Lead by Example

Leaders and managers have a significant impact on the psychological safety of their teams. By demonstrating open and non-judgmental communication, actively listening to employees, and valuing diverse perspectives, leaders can set the tone for psychological safety within the organization. Encourage leaders to share their own vulnerabilities and mistakes, creating a culture that embraces learning and growth.

6.1.2.2 Establish Clear Expectations

Clearly communicate expectations regarding respectful and inclusive behavior to all employees. This includes promoting active listening, empathy, and constructive feedback. By setting these expectations, employees understand the importance of psychological safety and are more likely to uphold these values in their interactions.

Building trust and respect is fundamental to creating psychological safety. Encourage team-building activities, promote collaboration, and provide opportunities for employees to get to know one another on a personal level. This helps to establish a sense of trust and camaraderie, making it easier for individuals to express themselves openly.

6.1.2.4 Encourage Open Communication and Feedback

Create channels for open communication and feedback within the organization. This can include regular team meetings, suggestion boxes, or anonymous feedback mechanisms. Encourage employees to share their thoughts, ideas, and concerns without fear of judgment or reprisal. Actively listen to their feedback and take appropriate action to address any issues raised.

6.1.2.5 Promote Diversity and Inclusion

A diverse and inclusive workplace is essential for psychological safety. Embrace diversity in all its forms and create an inclusive culture where everyone feels valued and respected. Encourage the participation of individuals from different backgrounds, experiences, and perspectives in decision-making processes. This fosters a sense of belonging and psychological safety for all employees.

6.1.3 Benefits of Psychological Safety

Promoting psychological safety within the workplace has numerous benefits for both employees and the organization as a whole. Some of these benefits include:

1. Increased innovation and creativity: When employees feel safe to share their ideas, organizations can tap into a wider range of perspectives, leading to more innovative solutions and approaches.

2. Improved problem-solving and decision-making: Psychological safety encourages open and honest communication, allowing for more effective problem-solving and decision-making processes. Different viewpoints and ideas can be explored without fear of judgment or criticism.

3. Enhanced employee engagement and satisfaction: When employees feel psychologically safe, they are more engaged in their work and have higher levels of job satisfaction. This leads to increased productivity, lower turnover rates, and a positive work culture.

4. Better teamwork and collaboration: Psychological safety fosters a sense of trust and respect among team members, leading to improved collaboration and teamwork. This results in higher-quality outcomes and stronger working relationships.

5. Reduced stress and improved well-being: A psychologically safe work environment reduces stress levels and promotes employee well-being. When individuals feel safe and supported, they are better able to manage stress and maintain a healthy work-life balance.

Conclusion

Psychological safety is a critical component of creating an aware corporate culture. As a psychologist, understanding the importance of psychological safety and implementing strategies to foster it within the workplace is essential. By promoting open communication, trust, respect, and diversity, you can help create a safe and supportive work environment where employees can thrive, contribute their best, and experience overall well-being.

6.2 Creating a Safe and Supportive Work Environment

Creating a safe and supportive work environment is crucial for promoting employee well-being and fostering a positive corporate culture. As a psychologist, your role in this process is vital, as you can provide valuable insights and guidance to organizations on how to create an environment that prioritizes psychological safety and supports the overall well-being of employees.

6.2.1 Understanding Psychological Safety

Psychological safety refers to the belief that one can express their thoughts, ideas, and concerns without fear of negative consequences such as ridicule, rejection, or punishment. It is a fundamental aspect of a safe and supportive work environment. When employees feel psychologically safe, they are more likely to engage in open communication, take risks, and contribute to the organization's success.

As a psychologist, you can help organizations understand the importance of psychological safety and its impact on employee well-being and performance. By conducting assessments and surveys, you can identify areas where psychological safety may be lacking and work with leadership to address these issues.

6.2.2 Creating a Culture of Psychological Safety

To create a safe and supportive work environment, it is essential to establish a culture of psychological safety throughout the organization. This involves fostering an atmosphere where employees feel comfortable speaking up, sharing their ideas, and challenging the status quo without fear of retribution.

As a psychologist, you can collaborate with organizational leaders to develop strategies and initiatives that promote psychological safety. This may include:

1. **Leadership modeling**: Encouraging leaders to demonstrate vulnerability, openness, and active listening. When leaders lead by example and show that they value and respect diverse perspectives, it sets the tone for the entire organization.

2. **Training and education**: Providing training programs and workshops to enhance employees' understanding of psychological safety and its importance. These programs can help employees develop the skills and knowledge necessary to create a safe and supportive work environment.

3. **Clear communication channels**: Establishing clear and accessible channels for employees to voice their concerns, provide feedback, and seek support. This can include regular team meetings, suggestion boxes, or anonymous reporting systems.

4. **Conflict resolution processes**: Implementing effective conflict resolution processes that encourage open dialogue and facilitate the resolution of conflicts in a fair and respectful manner. This can help prevent conflicts from escalating and create an environment where differences are embraced and resolved constructively.

5. **Recognition and appreciation**: Recognizing and appreciating employees' contributions and efforts. Celebrating achievements and acknowledging the value of diverse perspectives can foster a sense of belonging and encourage employees to continue sharing their ideas and opinions.

6.2.3 Encouraging Open Communication and Feedback

Open communication and feedback are essential components of a safe and supportive work environment. They enable employees to express their thoughts, concerns, and suggestions, fostering a culture of trust and collaboration. As a psychologist, you can assist organizations in implementing strategies to encourage open communication and feedback, such as:

1. **Active listening**: Encouraging active listening skills among employees and leaders. This involves giving full attention to the speaker, seeking clarification, and demonstrating empathy. Active listening promotes understanding and helps build stronger relationships within the organization.

2. **Regular feedback sessions**: Establishing regular feedback sessions between employees and their supervisors. These sessions provide an opportunity for employees to discuss their progress, receive constructive feedback, and address any concerns or challenges they may be facing.

3. **360-degree feedback**: Implementing a 360-degree feedback process where employees receive feedback from their peers, subordinates, and supervisors. This comprehensive feedback approach provides a holistic view of an employee's performance and encourages open and honest communication.

4. **Anonymous feedback mechanisms**: Creating anonymous feedback mechanisms, such as surveys or suggestion boxes, to allow employees to express their opinions and concerns without fear of reprisal. This can help uncover issues that may otherwise go unnoticed and provide valuable insights for organizational improvement.

6.2.4 Addressing and Resolving Conflict

Conflict is inevitable in any workplace, but how it is addressed and resolved can significantly impact the overall work environment. As a psychologist, you can play a crucial role in helping organizations address and resolve conflicts in a constructive and respectful manner. Some strategies to consider include:

1. **Mediation and facilitation**: Acting as a mediator or facilitator in conflict resolution processes. Your expertise in communication and conflict resolution techniques can help parties involved in a conflict find common ground, understand each other's perspectives, and work towards a mutually beneficial resolution.

2. **Conflict management training**: Providing conflict management training to employees and leaders. This training can equip individuals with the skills and strategies necessary to manage conflicts effectively, including active listening, empathy, negotiation, and compromise.

3. **Establishing conflict resolution policies**: Assisting organizations in developing clear conflict resolution policies and procedures. These policies should outline the steps to be taken when conflicts arise, ensuring that conflicts are addressed promptly and fairly.

4. **Promoting a culture of respect**: Emphasizing the importance of respect and professionalism in the workplace. By promoting a culture where differences are valued and respected, organizations can minimize the occurrence of conflicts and create an environment where conflicts are resolved in a healthy and constructive manner.

By actively promoting a safe and supportive work environment, you can contribute to the overall well-being and success of employees and the organization as a whole. Your role as a psychologist in creating awareness and implementing strategies for psychological safety, open communication, and conflict resolution is invaluable in shaping a positive corporate culture.

Open communication and feedback are essential components of a healthy and aware corporate culture. When employees feel comfortable expressing their thoughts, concerns, and ideas, it fosters a sense of trust, collaboration, and engagement within the organization. As a psychologist, your role in creating an aware corporate culture is to encourage and facilitate open communication and feedback among employees at all levels.

6.3.1 The Importance of Open Communication

Open communication is the foundation of a transparent and inclusive work environment. It allows for the free flow of information, ideas, and feedback, which can lead to improved problem-solving, innovation, and overall organizational performance. When employees feel heard and valued, they are more likely to be motivated, engaged, and committed to their work.

Encouraging open communication also helps to prevent misunderstandings, conflicts, and the spread of rumors. By promoting a culture of open dialogue, you can create an environment where employees feel comfortable expressing their opinions, seeking clarification, and addressing any concerns they may have.

6.3.2 Creating Channels for Communication

As a psychologist, you can play a crucial role in creating channels for communication within the organization. This involves establishing various platforms and mechanisms that facilitate the exchange of information and ideas. Some effective strategies include:

1. **Regular team meetings:** Encourage managers to hold regular team meetings where employees can share updates, discuss challenges, and provide feedback. These meetings should be inclusive and provide a safe space for open dialogue.

2. **Town hall meetings:** Organize town hall meetings where employees have the opportunity to ask questions, voice concerns, and provide suggestions directly to senior leaders. This promotes transparency and allows for direct communication between employees and management.

3. **Online platforms:** Implement online platforms, such as intranet portals or collaboration tools, where employees can share ideas, ask questions, and provide feedback. These platforms can also serve as a knowledge-sharing hub and foster collaboration across different teams and departments.

4. **Anonymous feedback channels:** Establish anonymous feedback channels, such as suggestion boxes or online surveys, to encourage employees who may be hesitant to speak up openly. This allows for honest feedback without fear of retribution.

6.3.3 Active Listening and Empathy

To create an environment conducive to open communication, it is important to practice active listening and empathy. As a psychologist, you can help employees feel heard and understood by:

1. **Being present:** When engaging in conversations, give your full attention to the speaker. Maintain eye contact, nod to show understanding, and avoid distractions.

2. **Empathizing:** Show empathy by acknowledging and validating the speaker's feelings and experiences. This helps build trust and encourages further sharing.

3. **Asking open-ended questions:** Encourage employees to elaborate on their thoughts and feelings by asking open-ended questions. This

demonstrates your genuine interest in understanding their perspective.

4. **Reflecting and summarizing:** Summarize and reflect what the speaker has shared to ensure accurate understanding. This also shows that you are actively listening and processing the information.

Feedback is a vital component of open communication and continuous improvement. As a psychologist, you can help employees and managers provide constructive feedback by:

1. **Focusing on behavior and impact:** Encourage individuals to provide feedback based on specific behaviors and their impact on the work environment or team dynamics. This helps to keep the feedback objective and actionable.

2. **Using the "sandwich" approach:** When delivering feedback, use the "sandwich" approach by starting with positive feedback, providing constructive criticism, and ending with positive reinforcement. This helps to balance the feedback and maintain a supportive tone.

3. **Encouraging two-way feedback:** Emphasize the importance of two-way feedback, where both the giver and receiver have the opportunity to share their perspectives. This promotes a culture of mutual respect and continuous learning.

4. **Offering guidance and support:** Provide guidance and support to individuals who may struggle with giving or receiving feedback. This can include coaching sessions, workshops, or resources on effective feedback techniques.

Open communication and feedback can sometimes lead to conflicts within the workplace. As a psychologist, you can assist in resolving conflicts and mediating disputes by:

1. **Creating a safe space:** Establish a safe and neutral environment where conflicting parties can openly express their concerns and perspectives without fear of judgment or retaliation.

2. **Acting as a mediator:** Serve as a mediator to facilitate open dialogue between conflicting parties. Encourage active listening, empathy, and a focus on finding mutually beneficial solutions.

3. **Teaching conflict resolution skills:** Provide training and workshops on conflict resolution skills, such as effective communication, negotiation, and problem-solving. This equips employees with the tools they need to address conflicts in a constructive manner.

4. **Promoting a culture of forgiveness and reconciliation:** Encourage a culture of forgiveness and reconciliation by emphasizing the importance of understanding, empathy, and finding common ground. This helps to rebuild relationships and maintain a positive work environment.

By encouraging open communication and feedback, you can help create an aware corporate culture that values transparency, collaboration, and continuous improvement. Your role as a psychologist is to facilitate and support these communication processes, ensuring that employees feel heard, valued, and empowered to contribute to the organization's success.

CHAPTER VII

THE ROLE OF EMOTIONAL INTELLIGENCE IN WORKPLACE WELL-BEING

Emotional intelligence (EI) is a crucial aspect of workplace well-being and plays a significant role in creating a positive and healthy corporate culture. It refers to the ability to recognize, understand, and manage our own emotions, as well as the emotions of others. In the context of the workplace, emotional intelligence involves using emotional information to guide thinking and behavior, fostering effective communication, and building strong relationships.

7.1.1 The Components of Emotional Intelligence

Emotional intelligence consists of several components that contribute to an individual's ability to navigate and thrive in the workplace. These components include:

1. **Self-awareness**: This involves recognizing and understanding one's own emotions, strengths, weaknesses, and values. Self-aware individuals are better equipped to manage their emotions and make informed decisions.

2. **Self-regulation**: Self-regulation refers to the ability to control and manage one's emotions, impulses, and behaviors. It involves being adaptable, resilient, and able to handle stress effectively.

3. **Motivation**: Motivation is the drive to achieve goals and the ability to persevere in the face of challenges. Emotionally intelligent individuals are often self-motivated, have a strong work ethic, and are committed to personal and professional growth.

4. **Empathy**: Empathy is the ability to understand and share the feelings of others. It involves being able to put oneself in another person's shoes and respond with compassion and understanding.

5. **Social skills**: Social skills encompass a range of abilities, including effective communication, conflict

resolution, teamwork, and leadership. Emotionally intelligent individuals excel in building and maintaining positive relationships with colleagues and clients.

Emotional intelligence is increasingly recognized as a critical factor in workplace success and well-being. Research has shown that individuals with high emotional intelligence are more likely to experience job satisfaction, have better mental health, and perform well in their roles. Here are some key reasons why emotional intelligence is important in the workplace:

1. **Enhanced communication**: Emotionally intelligent individuals are skilled communicators. They can express themselves clearly, listen actively, and understand the emotions underlying others' messages. This leads to improved collaboration, reduced misunderstandings, and stronger relationships within teams.

2. **Effective leadership**: Leaders with high emotional intelligence are more likely to inspire and motivate their teams. They can understand and respond to the needs and emotions of their employees, creating a supportive and engaging work environment.

3. **Conflict resolution**: Emotional intelligence plays a crucial role in resolving conflicts constructively. Individuals with high emotional intelligence can manage their own emotions during conflicts and understand the perspectives of others. This enables them to find mutually beneficial solutions and maintain positive working relationships.

4. **Stress management**: The ability to regulate emotions and manage stress is essential in today's fast-paced work environments. Emotionally

intelligent individuals are better equipped to handle workplace pressures, adapt to change, and maintain their well-being.

5. **Teamwork and collaboration**: Emotional intelligence fosters effective teamwork and collaboration. Individuals who can understand and respond to the emotions of their team members can build trust, promote cooperation, and create a positive team dynamic.

7.1.3 Developing Emotional Intelligence in Employees

As a psychologist, you play a crucial role in helping individuals develop and enhance their emotional intelligence. Here are some strategies to promote emotional intelligence in the workplace:

1. **Assessment and feedback**: Conduct assessments to measure employees' emotional intelligence levels and provide them with feedback. This can help individuals identify their strengths and areas for improvement.

2. **Training and workshops**: Offer training programs and workshops that focus on developing emotional intelligence skills. These sessions can provide employees with practical tools and techniques to enhance their self-awareness, self-regulation, empathy, and social skills.

3. **Coaching and mentoring**: Provide one-on-one coaching or mentoring sessions to support employees in their emotional intelligence development. This personalized approach can help individuals apply emotional intelligence principles to their specific roles and challenges.

4. **Promote self-reflection**: Encourage employees to engage in self-reflection and self-assessment of their emotions, behaviors, and interactions with

others. This can help them gain insights into their emotional patterns and make conscious efforts to improve their emotional intelligence.

5. **Model emotional intelligence**: As a psychologist, it is essential to model emotional intelligence in your own interactions and behaviors. By demonstrating empathy, active listening, and effective communication, you can inspire and encourage employees to develop their emotional intelligence.

Emotional intelligence is particularly valuable in conflict resolution and teamwork. Here's how it can be applied in these contexts:

1. **Conflict resolution**: Emotionally intelligent individuals can approach conflicts with empathy and understanding. They can manage their own emotions and remain calm during tense situations. By actively listening to all parties involved and considering their perspectives, emotionally intelligent individuals can find mutually beneficial solutions and foster positive relationships.

2. **Teamwork**: Emotional intelligence is crucial for building strong and cohesive teams. Emotionally intelligent team members can understand and respond to the emotions of their colleagues, fostering trust, collaboration, and effective communication. They can also navigate conflicts within the team and promote a positive team culture.

By understanding emotional intelligence and its significance in the workplace, psychologists can play a vital role in helping individuals and organizations create a culture that values and promotes emotional intelligence. Through assessments, training, coaching, and modeling, psychologists can support employees in developing their emotional intelligence skills, leading to improved well-being, productivity, and overall success in the workplace.

7.2 Developing Emotional Intelligence in Employees

Emotional intelligence (EI) plays a crucial role in creating a positive and healthy work environment. As a psychologist, it is essential to understand the significance of emotional intelligence and its impact on employee well-being. Developing emotional intelligence in employees can lead to improved communication, enhanced teamwork, and better conflict resolution skills. In this section, we will explore the role of the psychologist in developing emotional intelligence in employees and the strategies that can be employed to foster emotional intelligence within the workplace.

7.2.1 Understanding Emotional Intelligence

Before delving into the development of emotional intelligence, it is important to have a clear understanding of what emotional intelligence entails. Emotional intelligence refers to the ability to recognize, understand, and manage one's own emotions, as well as the emotions of others. It involves being aware of one's emotions, having empathy for others, and effectively regulating emotions in various situations.

Emotional intelligence consists of several key components, including self-awareness, self-regulation, motivation, empathy, and social skills. Employees with high emotional intelligence are better equipped to handle stress, build positive relationships, and navigate conflicts effectively. By developing emotional intelligence, employees can enhance their overall well-being and contribute to a healthier work environment.

7.2.2 Assessing Emotional Intelligence

As a psychologist, one of the first steps in developing emotional intelligence in employees is to assess their current level of emotional intelligence. This can be done through various assessment tools and techniques. These assessments can provide valuable insights into an individual's strengths and areas for improvement in terms of emotional intelligence.

Some commonly used assessments include self-report questionnaires, behavioral observations, and feedback from colleagues and supervisors. These assessments can help identify specific areas where employees may need support and development. By understanding the emotional intelligence profiles of employees, psychologists can tailor interventions and strategies to meet their unique needs.

7.2.3 Training and Development Programs

Once the emotional intelligence of employees has been assessed, psychologists can design and implement training and development programs to enhance emotional intelligence skills. These programs can be conducted through workshops, seminars, or online platforms, depending on the organization's resources and preferences.

Training programs can focus on various aspects of emotional intelligence, such as self-awareness, self-regulation, empathy, and social skills. They can include activities and exercises that promote self-reflection, emotional regulation techniques, and role-playing scenarios to practice empathy and effective communication. By providing employees with the necessary knowledge and skills, psychologists can empower them to develop and apply emotional intelligence in their daily work interactions.

7.2.4 Coaching and Mentoring

In addition to training programs, psychologists can also provide individual coaching and mentoring to employees to further develop their emotional intelligence. Through one-on-one sessions, psychologists can offer personalized guidance and support to help employees identify and overcome emotional challenges.

Coaching sessions can focus on specific areas where employees may struggle, such as managing stress, handling conflicts, or building relationships. Psychologists can provide strategies and techniques to improve emotional intelligence in these areas and offer ongoing support as employees navigate their emotions in the workplace.

7.2.5 Promoting Emotional Intelligence in Leadership

Developing emotional intelligence is not limited to employees alone; it is equally important for leaders within the organization to possess high emotional intelligence. Psychologists can play a crucial role in promoting emotional intelligence among leaders by providing coaching, training, and feedback.

By enhancing emotional intelligence in leadership, psychologists can create a ripple effect throughout the organization. Leaders with high emotional intelligence can set a positive example for employees, foster a supportive work environment, and effectively manage conflicts. This, in turn, can contribute to the overall well-being and success of the organization.

7.2.6 Integrating Emotional Intelligence into Performance Management

To ensure the sustained development of emotional intelligence in employees, psychologists can work with the organization to integrate emotional intelligence into performance management processes. This can be done by incorporating emotional intelligence competencies into performance evaluations, goal setting, and development plans.

By linking emotional intelligence to performance management, employees are encouraged to continuously develop and apply their emotional intelligence skills. This integration sends a clear message that emotional intelligence is valued and recognized as an essential component of success within the organization.

7.2.7 Creating a Supportive Work Environment

Lastly, psychologists can collaborate with organizational leaders to create a supportive work environment that nurtures emotional intelligence. This can be achieved by fostering open communication, promoting psychological safety, and providing resources for employees to enhance their emotional well-being.

Psychologists can advocate for policies and practices that prioritize employee well-being and emotional intelligence. This may include flexible work arrangements, wellness programs, and opportunities for personal and professional development. By creating a supportive work environment, psychologists can contribute to the overall emotional intelligence and well-being of employees.

In conclusion, the development of emotional intelligence in employees is a vital aspect of creating a healthy and thriving work environment. Psychologists play a crucial role in assessing emotional intelligence, designing training programs, providing coaching, and promoting emotional intelligence in leadership. By integrating emotional intelligence into performance management and creating a supportive work environment, psychologists can contribute to the overall well-being and success of both individuals and organizations.

Conflict is an inevitable part of any workplace. Whether it's a disagreement between colleagues, a clash of personalities, or a difference in opinions, conflict can arise in various forms. However, how organizations handle and resolve these conflicts can significantly impact the overall well-being and productivity of their employees. This is where emotional intelligence and conflict resolution skills play a crucial role, and psychologists can provide valuable guidance and support in this area.

7.3.1 Understanding Emotional Intelligence

Emotional intelligence refers to the ability to recognize, understand, and manage our own emotions and the emotions of others. It involves being aware of our emotions, controlling them effectively, and using them to guide our thoughts and actions. Emotional intelligence is a vital skill in conflict resolution because it allows individuals to navigate difficult situations with empathy, understanding, and self-awareness.

Psychologists can help organizations develop emotional intelligence in their employees by providing training and workshops focused on emotional awareness, self-regulation, empathy, and effective communication. By enhancing emotional intelligence, employees can better understand their own emotions and the emotions of others, leading to more effective conflict resolution.

7.3.2 The Role of Emotional Intelligence in Conflict Resolution

Conflict resolution requires individuals to manage their emotions and communicate effectively to find mutually beneficial solutions. Emotional intelligence plays a significant role in this process by enabling individuals to:

Emotional intelligence helps individuals regulate their emotions during conflicts. It allows them to remain calm and composed, even in high-stress situations, which can prevent conflicts from escalating further. Psychologists can teach employees techniques for managing their emotions, such as deep breathing exercises, mindfulness practices, and cognitive reframing, to help them stay focused and rational during conflicts.

Conflict often arises from differing perspectives and opinions. Emotional intelligence enables individuals to understand and appreciate different viewpoints, fostering empathy and open-mindedness. Psychologists can facilitate exercises and discussions that encourage employees to see conflicts from multiple perspectives, helping them develop a broader understanding of the situation and promoting more constructive dialogue.

Effective communication is essential for resolving conflicts. Emotional intelligence allows individuals to express their thoughts and feelings assertively and respectfully, without resorting to aggression or passive-aggressive behavior. Psychologists can teach employees active listening skills, non-verbal communication techniques, and conflict resolution strategies that promote open and honest communication.

Emotional intelligence helps individuals collaborate and find mutually beneficial solutions during conflicts. By understanding their own emotions and the emotions of others, employees can work together to identify common goals and brainstorm creative solutions. Psychologists can facilitate team-building activities and problem-solving exercises that encourage collaboration and foster a positive conflict resolution environment.

7.3.3 Applying Emotional Intelligence in Conflict Resolution

Psychologists can assist organizations in applying emotional intelligence in conflict resolution by:

7.3.3.1 Providing Mediation and Facilitation

Psychologists can act as mediators or facilitators in conflict resolution processes. They can help create a safe and neutral space for employees to express their concerns, listen to each other, and work towards finding common ground. Through active listening, empathy, and effective communication techniques, psychologists can guide the parties involved in conflict towards a resolution that satisfies everyone's needs.

7.3.3.2 Training Conflict Resolution Skills

Psychologists can conduct training sessions to equip employees with conflict resolution skills. These sessions can cover topics such as active listening, assertive communication, negotiation techniques, and problem-solving strategies. By providing employees with the necessary tools and knowledge, psychologists empower them to handle conflicts more effectively and promote a positive work environment.

7.3.3.3 Promoting Emotional Intelligence in Leadership

Leaders play a crucial role in conflict resolution within organizations. Psychologists can work closely with leaders to enhance their emotional intelligence and conflict resolution skills. By developing self-awareness, empathy, and effective communication, leaders can set a positive example for their teams and create a culture that values open dialogue and constructive conflict resolution.

Psychologists can conduct conflict assessments within organizations to identify areas of concern and potential sources of conflict. These assessments can involve surveys, interviews, and observations to gather data on the nature and frequency of conflicts. By understanding the underlying causes of conflicts, psychologists can develop targeted interventions and strategies to address them effectively.

In conclusion, emotional intelligence plays a vital role in conflict resolution within the workplace. Psychologists can assist organizations in developing emotional intelligence in their employees, providing mediation and facilitation, training conflict resolution skills, promoting emotional intelligence in leadership, and conducting conflict assessments. By incorporating emotional intelligence into conflict resolution processes, organizations can create a more harmonious and productive work environment.

7.4 Using Emotional Intelligence to Enhance Teamwork

Emotional intelligence (EI) plays a crucial role in enhancing teamwork within an organization. As a psychologist, understanding and utilizing emotional intelligence can significantly contribute to creating a positive and productive work environment. In this section, we will explore how emotional intelligence can be used to enhance teamwork and foster collaboration among employees.

7.4.1 Understanding Emotional Intelligence in the Context of Teamwork

Emotional intelligence refers to the ability to recognize, understand, and manage our own emotions and the emotions of others. It involves being aware of our emotions, empathizing with others, and effectively communicating and resolving conflicts. When it comes to teamwork, emotional intelligence becomes even more critical as it directly impacts the dynamics and effectiveness of the team.

Teams that possess high emotional intelligence are more likely to experience increased trust, open communication, and collaboration. By understanding and managing their emotions, team members can build stronger relationships, resolve conflicts more effectively, and work towards common goals. As a psychologist, it is essential to promote emotional intelligence within teams to enhance their overall performance and well-being.

7.4.2 Developing Emotional Intelligence in Team Members

To enhance teamwork through emotional intelligence, psychologists can implement various strategies to develop and nurture emotional intelligence skills among team members. Here are some effective approaches:

7.4.2.1 Self-awareness

Encouraging team members to develop self-awareness is the first step towards enhancing emotional intelligence. Psychologists can facilitate activities and workshops that help individuals recognize and understand their own emotions, strengths, and weaknesses. By promoting self-reflection and introspection, team members can gain a deeper understanding of their emotional triggers and how they impact their interactions with others.

7.4.2.2 Empathy

Empathy is a crucial aspect of emotional intelligence that allows individuals to understand and share the feelings of others. Psychologists can organize empathy-building exercises and role-playing scenarios to help team members develop their empathetic skills. By encouraging team members to put themselves in others' shoes, psychologists can foster a sense of understanding and compassion within the team.

7.4.2.3 Effective communication

Clear and open communication is vital for successful teamwork. Psychologists can provide training and guidance on effective communication techniques, such as active listening, non-verbal cues, and assertiveness. By improving communication skills, team members can express their thoughts and emotions more effectively, leading to better collaboration and problem-solving.

7.4.2.4 Conflict resolution

Conflict is inevitable in any team setting. However, emotional intelligence can help team members navigate conflicts in a constructive manner. Psychologists can teach conflict resolution strategies, such as active listening, finding common ground, and seeking win-win solutions. By equipping team members with these skills, psychologists can promote a positive and supportive team environment where conflicts are resolved amicably.

7.4.3 Applying Emotional Intelligence to Teamwork

Once team members have developed their emotional intelligence skills, psychologists can guide them in applying these skills to enhance teamwork. Here are some ways emotional intelligence can be utilized:

7.4.3.1 Building trust

Trust is the foundation of effective teamwork. By utilizing emotional intelligence, team members can build trust by being open, honest, and reliable. Psychologists can facilitate trust-building exercises and encourage team members to share their thoughts and feelings openly. By fostering an environment of trust, team members will feel more comfortable collaborating and taking risks together.

Emotional intelligence enables team members to work collaboratively and cooperatively. By understanding and valuing each other's perspectives, team members can leverage their diverse skills and knowledge to achieve common goals. Psychologists can facilitate team-building activities that promote cooperation and encourage team members to appreciate the strengths and contributions of their colleagues.

7.4.3.3 Conflict management

Conflicts within a team can be detrimental if not managed effectively. Emotional intelligence allows team members to approach conflicts with empathy and understanding. Psychologists can guide team members in resolving conflicts by encouraging active listening, promoting open dialogue, and finding mutually beneficial solutions. By utilizing emotional intelligence, team members can transform conflicts into opportunities for growth and learning.

7.4.3.4 Emotional support

Teams that possess high emotional intelligence are more likely to provide emotional support to one another. Psychologists can foster a culture of emotional support by encouraging team members to be empathetic and compassionate towards their colleagues. By creating a safe space for expressing emotions and offering support, psychologists can enhance team cohesion and well-being.

Conclusion

Emotional intelligence is a powerful tool that psychologists can utilize to enhance teamwork and create a positive work environment. By developing emotional intelligence skills in team members and applying them to various aspects of teamwork, psychologists can foster collaboration, trust, and effective communication. Ultimately, utilizing emotional intelligence in the context of teamwork can lead to improved team performance, employee well-being, and organizational success.

CHAPTER VIII

THE PSYCHOLOGIST'S ROLE IN EMPLOYEE ENGAGEMENT

8.1 Understanding Employee Engagement

Employee engagement is a crucial aspect of creating a positive and productive work environment. It refers to the level of commitment, passion, and enthusiasm that employees have towards their work and the organization they work for. Engaged employees are more likely to be motivated, satisfied, and loyal, which ultimately leads to higher levels of productivity and well-being in the workplace.

As a psychologist, understanding employee engagement is essential in creating well-being in the workplace. By recognizing the factors that contribute to engagement and implementing strategies to enhance it, psychologists can play a significant role in fostering a positive and engaged workforce.

8.1.1 The Importance of Employee Engagement

Employee engagement is vital for several reasons. Firstly, engaged employees are more likely to be satisfied with their work, leading to higher levels of job performance and productivity. They are motivated to go above and beyond their job requirements, resulting in increased innovation and creativity within the organization.

Secondly, engaged employees are more likely to stay with the organization for a longer duration. High employee turnover can be costly for organizations in terms of recruitment, training, and lost productivity. By focusing on employee engagement, psychologists can help reduce turnover rates and retain valuable talent within the organization.

Furthermore, engaged employees are more likely to have positive relationships with their colleagues and supervisors. This fosters a supportive and collaborative work environment, leading to improved teamwork and overall organizational success.

8.1.2 Measuring and Assessing Employee Engagement

To effectively enhance employee engagement, psychologists must first measure and assess the current level of engagement within the organization. This can be done through various methods, including surveys, interviews, and focus groups.

Surveys are a commonly used tool to measure employee engagement. These surveys typically consist of a series of questions that assess different aspects of engagement, such as job satisfaction, motivation, and commitment. The results of these surveys provide valuable insights into the level of engagement within the organization and help identify areas for improvement.

In addition to surveys, psychologists can also conduct interviews and focus groups to gain a deeper understanding of employee engagement. These qualitative methods allow for more in-depth discussions and provide valuable insights into the underlying factors that contribute to engagement or disengagement.

8.1.3 Strategies for Increasing Employee Engagement

Once the level of employee engagement has been assessed, psychologists can develop strategies to enhance engagement within the organization. Here are some effective strategies that psychologists can employ:

1. Enhancing Communication and Feedback Channels

Open and transparent communication is essential for fostering employee engagement. Psychologists can work with organizational leaders to establish effective communication channels, such as regular team meetings, one-on-one check-ins, and anonymous suggestion boxes. These channels provide employees with opportunities to voice their opinions, concerns, and ideas, making them feel valued and heard.

Feedback is another crucial aspect of employee engagement. Psychologists can help implement feedback mechanisms, such as performance evaluations and 360-degree feedback, to provide employees with constructive feedback on their work. This not only helps employees understand their strengths and areas for improvement but also demonstrates that their contributions are recognized and valued.

2. Providing Opportunities for Growth and Development

Employees are more likely to be engaged when they have opportunities for growth and development. Psychologists can collaborate with organizational leaders to design training programs, mentorship initiatives, and career development plans. These initiatives help employees acquire new skills, enhance their knowledge, and advance their careers within the organization. By investing in employee development, psychologists can foster a sense of purpose and commitment among employees.

3. Recognizing and Rewarding Employee Contributions

Recognizing and rewarding employee contributions is a powerful way to enhance engagement. Psychologists can assist in developing recognition programs that acknowledge and appreciate employees' efforts and achievements. This can include employee of the month awards, public recognition in team meetings, or monetary incentives for exceptional performance. By recognizing and rewarding employees, psychologists can reinforce positive behaviors and motivate employees to continue performing at their best.

4. Promoting Work-Life Balance

Work-life balance is crucial for employee well-being and engagement. Psychologists can work with organizational leaders to implement policies and practices that support work-life balance, such as flexible work hours, remote work options, and wellness programs. By promoting work-life balance, psychologists can help employees manage their personal and professional responsibilities, reducing stress and enhancing engagement.

8.1.4 Maintaining and Sustaining Employee Engagement

Employee engagement is not a one-time effort but an ongoing process. Psychologists play a vital role in maintaining and sustaining employee engagement within the organization. Here are some strategies psychologists can employ:

1. Regularly Assessing Employee Engagement

To ensure that engagement levels remain high, psychologists should regularly assess employee engagement within the organization. This can be done through follow-up surveys, focus groups, or individual interviews. By continuously monitoring engagement levels, psychologists can identify any potential issues or areas for improvement and take proactive measures to address them.

2. Providing Support and Resources

Psychologists can provide ongoing support and resources to employees to help them maintain their engagement. This can include offering counseling services, stress management workshops, or career coaching. By providing these resources, psychologists can help employees navigate challenges and maintain their motivation and commitment to their work.

3. Encouraging Employee Involvement and Empowerment

Psychologists can encourage employee involvement and empowerment by promoting a participative decision-making process. This involves involving employees in decision-making processes, seeking their input and feedback, and empowering them to take ownership of their work. By involving employees in decision-making, psychologists can enhance their sense of belonging and commitment to the organization.

4. Celebrating Successes and Milestones

Celebrating successes and milestones is an effective way to maintain and sustain employee engagement. Psychologists can work with organizational leaders to create a culture of celebration, where achievements and milestones are recognized and celebrated. This can include team celebrations, awards ceremonies, or public acknowledgments. By celebrating successes, psychologists can reinforce positive behaviors and motivate employees to continue their engagement.

In conclusion, employee engagement is a critical factor in creating well-being in the workplace. As psychologists, understanding employee engagement and implementing strategies to enhance it is essential in fostering a positive and productive work environment. By measuring and assessing engagement levels, developing effective strategies, and maintaining engagement over time, psychologists can play a significant role in creating a culture of engagement and well-being within organizations.

8.2 Measuring and Assessing Employee Engagement

Employee engagement is a crucial aspect of creating a positive and productive work environment. It refers to the level of commitment, motivation, and involvement that employees have towards their work and the organization as a whole. Engaged employees are more likely to be satisfied, productive, and loyal, which ultimately contributes to the overall success of the organization. As a psychologist, it is essential to measure and assess employee engagement to understand the current state and identify areas for improvement. This section will explore various methods and strategies for measuring and assessing employee engagement.

One of the most common and effective ways to measure employee engagement is through surveys and questionnaires. These tools allow organizations to gather quantitative and qualitative data about employees' perceptions, attitudes, and experiences in the workplace. Surveys can be designed to assess various aspects of engagement, such as job satisfaction, commitment, motivation, and organizational culture.

When developing surveys, it is crucial to include a mix of closed-ended and open-ended questions. Closed-ended questions provide respondents with predefined response options, allowing for easy data analysis and comparison. On the other hand, open-ended questions allow employees to provide detailed feedback and insights, providing a deeper understanding of their engagement levels.

To ensure the validity and reliability of survey results, it is essential to use standardized and validated measurement scales. These scales have been rigorously tested and proven to accurately measure employee engagement. Examples of widely used scales include the Gallup Q12 survey, which assesses twelve key elements of engagement, and the Utrecht Work Engagement Scale, which measures vigor, dedication, and absorption.

In addition to surveys, focus groups and interviews can provide valuable qualitative data about employee engagement. These methods allow for in-depth discussions and exploration of employees' thoughts, feelings, and experiences. By facilitating open and honest conversations, psychologists can gain deeper insights into the factors that influence engagement within the organization.

Focus groups typically involve a small group of employees who share their perspectives on various engagement-related topics. The psychologist acts as a facilitator, guiding the discussion and encouraging participants to express their thoughts and ideas. Focus groups can uncover underlying issues, identify patterns, and generate ideas for improving engagement.

Individual interviews provide an opportunity for employees to share their experiences and concerns in a one-on-one setting. This method allows for more personal and confidential conversations, enabling employees to express themselves freely. Psychologists can use structured or semi-structured interview guides to ensure consistency while allowing flexibility for employees to elaborate on specific topics.

8.2.3 Observations and Behavioral Assessments

Observations and behavioral assessments can provide valuable insights into employee engagement by examining their actions, interactions, and behaviors in the workplace. Psychologists can observe employees' level of enthusiasm, collaboration, and commitment to their work. By observing team dynamics and interactions, psychologists can identify signs of engagement or disengagement.

Behavioral assessments can also be conducted through performance evaluations and feedback sessions. By evaluating employees' performance, psychologists can gain insights into their level of motivation, commitment, and overall engagement. Additionally, feedback sessions provide an opportunity for employees to discuss their goals, challenges, and aspirations, allowing psychologists to assess their level of engagement and provide support where needed.

8.2.4 Data Analysis and Metrics

Once data from surveys, focus groups, interviews, and observations have been collected, psychologists can analyze the information to gain a comprehensive understanding of employee engagement. Data analysis techniques such as descriptive statistics, correlation analysis, and thematic analysis can be used to identify patterns, trends, and relationships within the data.

Psychologists can also develop engagement metrics and key performance indicators (KPIs) to track and monitor engagement levels over time. These metrics can include employee turnover rates, absenteeism rates, productivity levels, and employee satisfaction scores. By regularly measuring and analyzing these metrics, psychologists can assess the effectiveness of engagement initiatives and identify areas that require improvement.

8.2.5 Benchmarking and Comparative Analysis

To gain a broader perspective on employee engagement, psychologists can also conduct benchmarking and comparative analysis. This involves comparing engagement levels within the organization to industry standards or best practices. By benchmarking against other organizations, psychologists can identify areas where their organization excels or falls behind, providing insights for improvement.

Psychologists can also compare engagement levels across different departments, teams, or job roles within the organization. This comparative analysis can help identify factors that contribute to higher or lower engagement levels in specific areas. By understanding these differences, psychologists can develop targeted strategies to improve engagement where it is most needed.

In conclusion, measuring and assessing employee engagement is crucial for psychologists in their role of creating well-being in the workplace. Surveys, focus groups, interviews, observations, and data analysis provide valuable insights into employees' level of commitment, motivation, and involvement. By understanding the current state of engagement and identifying areas for improvement, psychologists can develop effective strategies to enhance employee engagement and create a positive and productive work environment.

Employee engagement is a crucial aspect of creating a positive and productive work environment. When employees are engaged, they are more committed to their work, motivated to perform at their best, and have a higher level of job satisfaction. As a psychologist, there are several strategies you can employ to increase employee engagement within an organization.

8.3.1 Fostering a Positive Work Environment

Creating a positive work environment is essential for increasing employee engagement. As a psychologist, you can play a vital role in fostering this environment by promoting open communication, trust, and collaboration among employees. Encourage managers and leaders to create a supportive atmosphere where employees feel valued and appreciated for their contributions.

One effective strategy is to implement recognition and reward programs. Recognizing and rewarding employees for their achievements and efforts can significantly boost their engagement levels. This can be done through verbal praise, certificates, or even small tokens of appreciation. By acknowledging and celebrating their accomplishments, employees feel motivated and engaged in their work.

8.3.2 Providing Opportunities for Growth and Development

Employees are more likely to be engaged when they have opportunities for growth and development within the organization. As a psychologist, you can work with leaders and managers to create a culture that supports continuous learning and professional development.

Encourage the implementation of training programs, workshops, and seminars that enhance employees' skills and knowledge. These opportunities not only help employees improve their performance but also demonstrate that the organization is invested in their growth. Additionally, consider implementing mentorship programs where experienced employees can guide and support their colleagues, fostering a sense of community and growth.

8.3.3 Empowering Employees

Empowering employees is another effective strategy for increasing engagement. When employees feel empowered, they have a sense of ownership and control over their work, leading to increased motivation and engagement. As a psychologist, you can help leaders and managers create an environment that encourages autonomy and decision-making.

Encourage leaders to delegate responsibilities and provide employees with the authority to make decisions within their roles. This not only increases engagement but also fosters a sense of trust and confidence in employees' abilities. Additionally, involve employees in decision-making processes and seek their input on matters that affect their work. This involvement creates a sense of ownership and investment in the organization's success.

8.3.4 Promoting Work-Life Balance

Work-life balance is crucial for employee engagement and overall well-being. As a psychologist, you can advocate for policies and practices that support work-life balance within the organization. Encourage leaders to promote flexible work arrangements, such as remote work options or flexible hours, to accommodate employees' personal needs.

Additionally, educate employees and managers about the importance of setting boundaries between work and personal life. Encourage employees to take breaks, use their vacation time, and prioritize self-care. By promoting work-life balance, employees will feel more engaged and satisfied with their work, leading to increased productivity and overall well-being.

8.3.5 Enhancing Communication and Feedback Channels

Effective communication and feedback channels are essential for increasing employee engagement. As a psychologist, you can help leaders and managers establish clear and open lines of communication throughout the organization.

Encourage regular team meetings, one-on-one check-ins, and feedback sessions to ensure that employees feel heard and valued. Provide training and guidance on effective communication techniques, such as active listening and constructive feedback. By fostering a culture of open communication, employees will feel more engaged and connected to the organization.

8.3.6 Encouraging Collaboration and Teamwork

Collaboration and teamwork are vital for employee engagement and organizational success. As a psychologist, you can facilitate team-building activities and promote a collaborative culture within the organization.

Encourage leaders to create cross-functional teams and provide opportunities for employees to work together on projects and initiatives. Foster a sense of camaraderie and cooperation by organizing team-building exercises, workshops, and social events. By promoting collaboration and teamwork, employees will feel more engaged and motivated to achieve shared goals.

8.3.7 Recognizing and Addressing Barriers to Engagement

It is essential to recognize and address any barriers to employee engagement within the organization. As a psychologist, you can conduct surveys, interviews, and focus groups to gather feedback from employees and identify potential obstacles.

Common barriers to engagement may include lack of communication, unclear expectations, limited growth opportunities, or excessive workload. Once these barriers are identified, work with leaders and managers to develop strategies to overcome them. This may involve implementing new policies, providing additional resources, or improving communication channels.

To ensure the effectiveness of engagement strategies, it is crucial to monitor and evaluate their impact regularly. As a psychologist, you can assist in designing and implementing surveys or assessments to measure employee engagement levels.

Analyze the data collected and identify trends or areas for improvement. Use this information to refine and adjust engagement initiatives as needed. By continuously monitoring and evaluating engagement efforts, organizations can maintain and sustain high levels of employee engagement.

In conclusion, as a psychologist, you play a vital role in increasing employee engagement within an organization. By fostering a positive work environment, providing growth opportunities, empowering employees, promoting work-life balance, enhancing communication and feedback channels, encouraging collaboration, addressing barriers, and monitoring initiatives, you can help create a workplace where employees are engaged, motivated, and fulfilled.

8.4 Maintaining and Sustaining Employee Engagement

Employee engagement is a crucial aspect of creating a positive and productive work environment. It refers to the level of commitment, enthusiasm, and involvement that employees have towards their work and the organization. As a psychologist, your role in maintaining and sustaining employee engagement is vital. By understanding the factors that contribute to engagement and implementing strategies to foster it, you can help create a workplace where employees feel valued, motivated, and connected to their work.

8.4.1 Understanding the Importance of Employee Engagement

Before delving into the strategies for maintaining and sustaining employee engagement, it is essential to understand why it is crucial for the overall well-being of the organization. Employee engagement has a direct impact on various aspects of the workplace, including productivity, job satisfaction, and employee retention. Engaged employees are more likely to go above and beyond their job requirements, contribute innovative ideas, and collaborate effectively with their colleagues. They also experience higher levels of job satisfaction and are less likely to leave the organization.

8.4.2 Creating a Supportive Work Environment

One of the key factors in maintaining and sustaining employee engagement is creating a supportive work environment. As a psychologist, you can contribute to this by promoting open communication, fostering positive relationships, and encouraging a culture of trust and respect. By creating an environment where employees feel safe to express their opinions, share their ideas, and voice their concerns, you can help build a strong foundation for engagement.

8.4.3 Providing Opportunities for Growth and Development

Employees are more likely to be engaged when they feel that their work is meaningful and that they have opportunities for growth and development. As a psychologist, you can play a crucial role in supporting employees' professional development by providing coaching, mentoring, and training programs. By helping employees identify their strengths and areas for improvement, you can assist them in setting goals and creating a development plan that aligns with their career aspirations. This not only enhances their skills and knowledge but also demonstrates the organization's commitment to their growth.

8.4.4 Recognizing and Rewarding Employee Contributions

Recognition and rewards are powerful tools for maintaining and sustaining employee engagement. As a psychologist, you can help design and implement recognition programs that acknowledge and appreciate employees' contributions. This can be done through formal recognition programs, such as employee of the month awards or performance-based bonuses, as well as informal recognition, such as verbal appreciation and thank-you notes. By recognizing and rewarding employees' efforts and achievements, you reinforce their sense of value and motivate them to continue performing at their best.

8.4.5 Promoting Work-Life Balance

Work-life balance is another critical factor in maintaining and sustaining employee engagement. As a psychologist, you can advocate for policies and practices that support work-life balance, such as flexible work arrangements, wellness programs, and time-off policies. By promoting a healthy work-life balance, you help employees manage their personal and professional responsibilities effectively, reducing stress and burnout. This, in turn, enhances their engagement and overall well-being.

8.4.6 Encouraging Employee Involvement and Empowerment

Engaged employees are those who feel a sense of ownership and empowerment in their work. As a psychologist, you can encourage employee involvement by providing opportunities for participation in decision-making processes, seeking their input on important matters, and involving them in problem-solving activities. By empowering employees to take ownership of their work and contribute to the organization's success, you foster a sense of pride and engagement.

8.4.7 Monitoring and Assessing Employee Engagement

To maintain and sustain employee engagement, it is essential to monitor and assess its levels regularly. As a psychologist, you can design and implement surveys, interviews, and focus groups to gather feedback from employees about their level of engagement and the factors that influence it. By analyzing this data, you can identify areas of improvement and develop targeted strategies to address any issues or concerns that may arise.

8.4.8 Continuous Improvement and Adaptation

Maintaining and sustaining employee engagement is an ongoing process that requires continuous improvement and adaptation. As a psychologist, you can play a crucial role in facilitating this process by staying updated on the latest research and best practices in employee engagement. By continuously evaluating and refining your strategies, you can ensure that they remain effective and relevant in the ever-changing workplace.

In conclusion, as a psychologist, your role in maintaining and sustaining employee engagement is multifaceted. By creating a supportive work environment, providing opportunities for growth and development, recognizing and rewarding employee contributions, promoting work-life balance, encouraging employee involvement and empowerment, monitoring and assessing engagement levels, and continuously improving your strategies, you can contribute to the creation of a highly engaged workforce. This, in turn, leads to increased productivity, job satisfaction, and overall well-being in the workplace.

CHAPTER IX

THE IMPACT OF WORK-LIFE BALANCE ON EMPLOYEE WELL-BEING

Work-life balance refers to the equilibrium between an individual's work responsibilities and their personal life. It is the ability to effectively manage and prioritize both professional and personal commitments, allowing individuals to have a fulfilling and satisfying life in and outside of the workplace. Achieving work-life balance is essential for overall well-being, as it helps to reduce stress, improve mental health, and enhance productivity.

In today's fast-paced and demanding work environments, work-life balance has become increasingly important. Many employees struggle to find the right balance between their work obligations and personal life, leading to feelings of overwhelm, burnout, and dissatisfaction. As a result, organizations are recognizing the significance of promoting work-life balance to support the well-being and productivity of their employees.

Work-life balance encompasses various aspects, including time management, flexibility, and the ability to disconnect from work. It involves allocating time and energy to different areas of life, such as family, hobbies, self-care, and social activities, in addition to work-related responsibilities. Achieving work-life balance is not about completely separating work and personal life, but rather finding a harmonious integration that allows individuals to thrive in both domains.

9.2 The Consequences of Work-Life Imbalance

Work-life balance is a crucial aspect of employee well-being and overall job satisfaction. When individuals are unable to effectively balance their work responsibilities with their personal lives, it can have significant consequences on their mental, emotional, and physical health. In this section, we will explore the various consequences of work-life imbalance and the negative impact it can have on both employees and organizations.

9.2.1 Increased Stress and Burnout

One of the most immediate consequences of work-life imbalance is increased stress levels. When individuals are constantly juggling multiple responsibilities and struggling to find time for themselves, it can lead to chronic stress. This stress can manifest in various ways, such as irritability, difficulty concentrating, and physical symptoms like headaches or insomnia.

Over time, prolonged stress can contribute to burnout, which is a state of physical, mental, and emotional exhaustion. Burnout can significantly impact an individual's ability to perform their job effectively and can lead to decreased productivity, increased absenteeism, and even long-term health issues.

9.2.2 Strained Relationships

Work-life imbalance can also take a toll on personal relationships. When individuals are constantly consumed by work and have little time or energy for their loved ones, it can lead to strained relationships and feelings of neglect. This can create tension, conflict, and a sense of isolation within the family unit.

Additionally, work-life imbalance can also impact social relationships outside of the family. When individuals are unable to participate in social activities or maintain friendships due to work commitments, it can lead to feelings of loneliness and a lack of social support.

9.2.3 Decreased Job Satisfaction

When work-life balance is compromised, job satisfaction often suffers as a result. Employees who feel overwhelmed by work demands and unable to find time for personal interests and activities may become disengaged and dissatisfied with their jobs. This can lead to decreased motivation, lower productivity, and an increased likelihood of seeking employment elsewhere.

Furthermore, work-life imbalance can also erode the sense of purpose and fulfillment that individuals derive from their work. When work becomes all-consuming and there is little time for personal growth or pursuing passions outside of work, individuals may begin to question the value and meaning of their professional lives.

9.2.4 Adverse Health Effects

The consequences of work-life imbalance extend beyond mental and emotional well-being and can have a significant impact on physical health as well. Chronic stress, which is often a result of work-life imbalance, has been linked to a variety of health problems, including cardiovascular disease, high blood pressure, and weakened immune function.

Additionally, when individuals are unable to prioritize self-care and engage in healthy lifestyle behaviors such as exercise, proper nutrition, and sufficient sleep, it can further contribute to the deterioration of their physical health. This can lead to increased sick leave, higher healthcare costs, and a decrease in overall well-being.

9.2.5 Reduced Organizational Performance

Work-life imbalance not only affects individual employees but also has implications for the overall performance of organizations. When employees are stressed, burned out, and dissatisfied with their jobs, it can lead to decreased productivity, lower quality of work, and increased turnover rates.

Furthermore, organizations that do not prioritize work-life balance may struggle to attract and retain top talent. In today's competitive job market, employees are increasingly seeking employers who value work-life balance and prioritize employee well-being. Failure to address work-life imbalance can result in a negative reputation for the organization and difficulty in recruiting and retaining skilled employees.

9.2.6 Impact on Work-Life Integration

In recent years, there has been a shift in focus from work-life balance to work-life integration. Work-life integration recognizes that work and personal life are not separate entities but rather interconnected aspects of an individual's overall well-being. Achieving work-life integration involves finding ways to effectively blend work and personal responsibilities, allowing individuals to thrive in both domains.

When work-life balance is not achieved, it becomes challenging to integrate work and personal life successfully. This can lead to a constant feeling of being pulled in multiple directions, difficulty in setting boundaries, and an inability to fully engage in either work or personal activities.

9.2.7 Impact on Organizational Culture

Work-life imbalance can also have a significant impact on organizational culture. When an organization does not prioritize work-life balance and fails to support employees in achieving it, it can create a culture of overwork, stress, and burnout. This can lead to a toxic work environment where employees feel undervalued, unsupported, and constantly under pressure.

On the other hand, organizations that prioritize work-life balance and create a supportive culture can foster employee well-being, satisfaction, and engagement. By promoting work-life balance, organizations can create a positive and healthy work environment that attracts and retains top talent, enhances productivity, and contributes to overall organizational success.

In conclusion, work-life imbalance can have severe consequences for both individuals and organizations. It can lead to increased stress, strained relationships, decreased job satisfaction, adverse health effects, reduced organizational performance, and a negative impact on organizational culture. Recognizing the importance of work-life balance and taking proactive steps to promote it is essential for creating a healthy and thriving workplace. As psychologists, it is our role to advocate for work-life balance and support individuals and organizations in achieving it.

Work-life balance is a crucial aspect of employee well-being and overall organizational success. It refers to the equilibrium between work-related responsibilities and personal life commitments. Achieving work-life balance is essential for employees to maintain their physical and mental health, enhance job satisfaction, and improve productivity. As a psychologist, you play a vital role in promoting work-life balance within the organization. By understanding the challenges employees face and implementing strategies to support them, you can contribute to creating a healthier and more productive work environment.

Before delving into the strategies for promoting work-life balance, it is essential to understand why it is crucial for both employees and the organization as a whole. Work-life balance has numerous benefits, including:

1. **Enhanced well-being**: When employees have a healthy balance between their work and personal life, they experience reduced stress levels, improved mental health, and increased overall well-being. This, in turn, leads to higher job satisfaction and better performance.

2. **Increased productivity**: Employees who have a good work-life balance are more focused, motivated, and energized. They are better able to manage their time, prioritize tasks, and maintain a high level of productivity. By promoting work-life balance, you can help employees avoid burnout and maintain their performance levels.

3. **Improved retention and recruitment**: Organizations that prioritize work-life balance are more attractive to potential employees. By offering flexible work arrangements and supporting employees' personal needs, organizations can attract and retain top talent. This, in turn, reduces turnover rates and saves the organization time and resources in recruiting and training new employees.

4. **Positive organizational culture**: A work environment that values work-life balance fosters a positive organizational culture. It demonstrates that the organization cares about its employees' well-being and encourages a healthy work-life integration. This, in turn, leads to higher employee engagement, satisfaction, and loyalty.

9.3.2 Strategies for Promoting Work-Life Balance

As a psychologist, you can implement various strategies to promote work-life balance within the organization. These strategies include:

1. **Flexible work arrangements**: Advocate for flexible work arrangements such as telecommuting, compressed workweeks, or flexible scheduling. These options allow employees to better manage their personal commitments while fulfilling their work responsibilities. Encourage managers and supervisors to be open to these arrangements and ensure that they are implemented fairly and consistently.

2. **Promote time management skills**: Provide training and resources to help employees improve their time management skills. This includes setting priorities, delegating tasks, and effectively managing their workload. By helping employees become more efficient and organized, they can better balance their work and personal life.

3.   **Encourage breaks and vacations**: Encourage employees to take regular breaks throughout the workday and utilize their vacation time. Promote the importance of disconnecting from work during non-working hours and encourage employees to fully recharge and rejuvenate. Lead by example and ensure that managers and supervisors support and encourage time off.

4.   **Create a supportive culture**: Foster a culture that values work-life balance and supports employees in achieving it. Encourage open communication and dialogue about work-life balance, and ensure that employees feel comfortable discussing their needs and concerns. Provide resources and support, such as employee assistance programs, to help employees navigate personal challenges that may impact their work-life balance.

5.   **Promote self-care**: Educate employees about the importance of self-care and provide resources to support their well-being. This can include workshops or seminars on stress management, mindfulness, and healthy lifestyle choices. Encourage employees to prioritize self-care activities such as exercise, hobbies, and spending time with loved ones.

6.   **Set realistic expectations**: Work with managers and supervisors to set realistic expectations for workload and deadlines. Avoid overloading employees with excessive work demands and ensure that they have the necessary resources and support to meet their responsibilities. Encourage open communication between employees and their supervisors to address any concerns or challenges related to work-life balance.

7.   **Monitor work-life balance**: Regularly assess and monitor the work-life balance within the

organization. This can be done through surveys, focus groups, or one-on-one discussions with employees. Use the feedback gathered to identify areas for improvement and develop targeted interventions to address work-life balance issues.

In addition to implementing strategies to promote work-life balance, it is essential to provide ongoing support to employees. As a psychologist, you can offer the following support:

1. **Individual counseling**: Provide individual counseling sessions to employees who are struggling with work-life balance. Help them identify strategies to manage their time, set boundaries, and prioritize their well-being. Offer guidance and support as they navigate personal and professional challenges.

2. **Workshops and training**: Conduct workshops and training sessions on work-life balance, stress management, and self-care. Provide employees with practical tools and techniques to achieve a healthy work-life balance. Offer resources and information on available support services within the organization.

3. **Manager and supervisor training**: Offer training programs for managers and supervisors on promoting work-life balance within their teams. Provide them with the skills and knowledge to support their employees' work-life balance needs effectively. Encourage them to lead by example and create a supportive work environment.

4. **Employee resource groups**: Establish employee resource groups focused on work-life balance and well-being. These groups can provide a platform for employees to share experiences, offer support, and

collaborate on initiatives to promote work-life balance within the organization.

5.   **Regular communication and feedback**: Maintain open lines of communication with employees and encourage them to provide feedback on work-life balance initiatives. Regularly assess the effectiveness of implemented strategies and make adjustments as needed. Ensure that employees feel heard and supported throughout the process.

By promoting work-life balance within the organization and providing ongoing support, you can contribute to creating a healthier and more productive work environment. Your role as a psychologist is crucial in helping employees achieve a balance between their work and personal life, leading to improved well-being and overall organizational success.

9.4 Supporting Employees in Achieving Work-Life Balance

Achieving work-life balance is essential for the well-being and overall satisfaction of employees. It is the responsibility of organizations to support their employees in finding a healthy equilibrium between their work and personal lives. In this section, we will explore the role of the psychologist in supporting employees in achieving work-life balance and the strategies they can employ to promote this balance.

9.4.1 Understanding the Importance of Work-Life Balance

Work-life balance refers to the equilibrium between the demands of work and personal life. It is crucial for individuals to have time and energy to devote to their personal relationships, hobbies, and self-care activities outside of work. When employees are able to achieve a healthy work-life balance, they experience reduced stress levels, improved mental and physical health, increased job satisfaction, and higher levels of productivity.

Psychologists play a vital role in identifying work-life imbalance among employees. They can conduct assessments and surveys to gauge the level of work-life balance within an organization. These assessments may include questions about the amount of time employees spend on work-related activities, their ability to disconnect from work during non-working hours, and their overall satisfaction with their work-life balance.

Psychologists can also observe behavioral and emotional indicators of work-life imbalance, such as increased stress, burnout, decreased job satisfaction, and strained personal relationships. By identifying these signs, psychologists can intervene and provide support to employees who are struggling to achieve work-life balance.

9.4.3 Providing Individual Counseling and Support

Psychologists can offer individual counseling and support to employees who are experiencing work-life imbalance. Through one-on-one sessions, psychologists can help employees identify the factors contributing to their imbalance and develop strategies to address them. This may involve setting boundaries, improving time management skills, and prioritizing self-care activities.

During counseling sessions, psychologists can also help employees explore their values and goals, both in their personal and professional lives. By aligning their actions with their values, employees can make conscious choices that promote work-life balance and overall well-being.

9.4.4 Facilitating Work-Life Balance Workshops and Training

Psychologists can organize workshops and training sessions to educate employees about the importance of work-life balance and provide them with practical strategies to achieve it. These workshops can cover topics such as time management, stress reduction techniques, setting boundaries, and effective communication skills.

Through interactive activities and group discussions, employees can learn from each other's experiences and gain valuable insights into achieving work-life balance. Psychologists can also provide resources and tools that employees can use to manage their time effectively and prioritize their personal well-being.

9.4.5 Collaborating with Managers and Leaders

Psychologists can collaborate with managers and leaders within the organization to create a supportive work environment that values work-life balance. They can provide training to managers on how to recognize and address work-life imbalance among their team members. This training can include strategies for delegating tasks, promoting flexible work arrangements, and fostering a culture of work-life balance.

Psychologists can also work with leaders to develop policies and practices that support work-life balance, such as flexible working hours, remote work options, and family-friendly benefits. By involving leaders in the process, psychologists can ensure that work-life balance is prioritized at all levels of the organization.

9.4.6 Promoting Self-Care and Well-being Initiatives

Psychologists can promote self-care and well-being initiatives within the organization to support employees in achieving work-life balance. They can organize wellness programs, such as yoga classes, mindfulness sessions, and stress management workshops, to help employees relax and recharge.

Additionally, psychologists can encourage employees to take regular breaks, practice self-care activities, and engage in hobbies outside of work. By promoting self-care, psychologists can help employees prioritize their well-being and create a healthier work-life balance.

9.4.7 Evaluating and Adjusting Work-Life Balance Strategies

Psychologists play a crucial role in evaluating the effectiveness of work-life balance strategies implemented within the organization. They can collect feedback from employees through surveys, focus groups, and individual interviews to assess the impact of these strategies on their work-life balance.

Based on the feedback received, psychologists can make adjustments to the strategies and interventions to better meet the needs of employees. This continuous evaluation and improvement process ensures that the organization remains responsive to the evolving work-life balance needs of its employees.

Conclusion

Achieving work-life balance is essential for the well-being and satisfaction of employees. Psychologists play a vital role in supporting employees in achieving this balance by providing individual counseling, facilitating workshops, collaborating with managers, promoting self-care initiatives, and evaluating the effectiveness of work-life balance strategies. By prioritizing work-life balance, organizations can create a healthier and more productive work environment for their employees.

CHAPTER X

THE ROLE OF THE PSYCHOLOGIST IN CONFLICT RESOLUTION

Workplace conflict is an inevitable part of any organization. It can arise due to differences in opinions, values, or goals among employees, or from external factors such as organizational changes or competition. Conflict can have a significant impact on employee well-being, job satisfaction, and overall productivity. Therefore, it is crucial for organizations to understand and effectively manage workplace conflict. This is where the role of a psychologist becomes essential.

10.1.1 The Importance of Understanding Workplace Conflict

Conflict in the workplace can have both positive and negative consequences. On one hand, it can lead to innovation, creativity, and growth. On the other hand, unresolved or poorly managed conflict can result in decreased employee morale, increased stress levels, and a toxic work environment. It is essential for organizations to recognize the importance of understanding workplace conflict in order to create a positive and productive work culture.

10.1.2 The Role of the Psychologist in Understanding Workplace Conflict

Psychologists play a crucial role in understanding workplace conflict and its underlying causes. They have the expertise to analyze the dynamics of conflict, identify its root causes, and develop strategies to effectively manage and resolve it. By understanding the psychological aspects of conflict, psychologists can provide valuable insights into the emotions, behaviors, and motivations of individuals involved in the conflict.

Psychologists can conduct thorough assessments to gain a comprehensive understanding of the conflict. They may use various methods such as interviews, surveys, and observations to gather information about the nature and extent of the conflict, the parties involved, and the underlying issues. This information helps psychologists develop tailored interventions and strategies to address the conflict effectively.

10.1.3 Conflict Resolution Strategies

Psychologists employ a range of conflict resolution strategies to help organizations manage workplace conflict. These strategies aim to promote open communication, understanding, and collaboration among employees. Some common conflict resolution strategies include:

10.1.3.1 Mediation

Mediation involves a neutral third party, often a psychologist, who facilitates communication and negotiation between conflicting parties. The mediator helps the parties identify their underlying interests, explore potential solutions, and reach a mutually acceptable agreement. Mediation can be particularly effective when there is a need for ongoing relationships between the parties involved.

10.1.3.2 Facilitation

Facilitation is a process in which a psychologist helps guide a group or team through a conflict resolution process. The psychologist ensures that all members have an opportunity to express their perspectives, encourages active listening, and facilitates the development of mutually beneficial solutions. Facilitation can be useful when conflicts arise within teams or departments.

10.1.3.3 Negotiation

Negotiation involves a process of give-and-take between conflicting parties to reach a mutually acceptable solution. Psychologists can assist in facilitating negotiations by helping parties identify their interests, explore potential trade-offs, and find common ground. Negotiation skills training can also be provided to employees to enhance their ability to resolve conflicts independently.

10.1.3.4 Training and Education

Psychologists can provide training and education to employees and managers on conflict resolution skills. This may include workshops or seminars on effective communication, active listening, problem-solving, and negotiation techniques. By equipping employees with these skills, organizations can empower them to address conflicts in a constructive and proactive manner.

10.1.4 Promoting Positive Conflict Resolution in the Organization

To create a culture of positive conflict resolution, organizations can implement several strategies with the guidance of psychologists. These strategies include:

10.1.4.1 Establishing Clear Communication Channels

Organizations should establish clear and open communication channels to encourage employees to express their concerns and resolve conflicts in a timely manner. This can include regular team meetings, suggestion boxes, or anonymous reporting systems. By providing employees with a safe and supportive environment to voice their concerns, organizations can prevent conflicts from escalating.

10.1.4.2 Encouraging Collaboration and Teamwork

Organizations should foster a culture of collaboration and teamwork, where employees are encouraged to work together towards common goals. By promoting a sense of shared purpose and emphasizing the value of diverse perspectives, organizations can reduce the likelihood of conflicts arising and encourage employees to resolve conflicts through constructive dialogue.

Organizations should develop and implement clear conflict resolution policies and procedures. These policies should outline the steps to be taken when conflicts arise, including the involvement of a psychologist or mediator if necessary. By providing employees with a structured framework for resolving conflicts, organizations can ensure consistency and fairness in the resolution process.

10.1.4.4 Promoting Emotional Intelligence

Emotional intelligence is the ability to recognize and manage one's own emotions and the emotions of others. Organizations can promote emotional intelligence by providing training and development opportunities that focus on self-awareness, empathy, and effective communication. By enhancing emotional intelligence in employees, organizations can facilitate better understanding and empathy, leading to more effective conflict resolution.

In conclusion, workplace conflict is a complex issue that can have a significant impact on employee well-being and organizational success. The role of a psychologist in understanding and managing workplace conflict is crucial. By employing various conflict resolution strategies and promoting positive conflict resolution practices, psychologists can help organizations create a healthy and productive work environment.

10.2 Conflict Resolution Strategies

Conflict is an inevitable part of any workplace, as individuals with different backgrounds, perspectives, and goals come together to work towards a common objective. However, if left unresolved, conflicts can escalate and negatively impact the overall well-being and productivity of employees. This is where the role of a psychologist becomes crucial in creating a harmonious and productive work environment. Psychologists possess the knowledge and skills to understand the underlying causes of conflicts and develop effective strategies for resolution.

10.2.1 Understanding the Nature of Conflict

Before delving into conflict resolution strategies, it is important to understand the nature of conflict in the workplace. Conflict can arise due to various reasons, such as differences in opinions, values, or goals, competition for resources, or interpersonal issues. It can manifest in different forms, including verbal arguments, passive-aggressive behavior, or even complete avoidance of communication. By recognizing the different types and sources of conflict, psychologists can tailor their strategies to address the specific needs of the organization and its employees.

10.2.2 Effective Communication and Active Listening

One of the fundamental strategies for resolving conflicts is effective communication. Psychologists can help employees and leaders develop strong communication skills, which are essential for expressing concerns, understanding different perspectives, and finding common ground. This involves teaching active listening techniques, such as paraphrasing, summarizing, and asking clarifying questions. By fostering open and respectful communication, psychologists can create an environment where conflicts can be addressed constructively.

10.2.3 Collaboration and Compromise

Collaboration and compromise are key elements in resolving conflicts. Psychologists can guide employees and leaders in finding win-win solutions that meet the needs and interests of all parties involved. This may involve facilitating brainstorming sessions, encouraging creative problem-solving, and helping individuals see beyond their own positions. By promoting a collaborative approach, psychologists can foster a sense of teamwork and unity, which can lead to more effective conflict resolution.

10.2.4 Mediation and Facilitation

In situations where conflicts become more complex or intense, psychologists can act as mediators or facilitators. Mediation involves a neutral third party assisting the conflicting parties in reaching a mutually acceptable resolution. Psychologists can facilitate the mediation process by creating a safe and supportive environment, ensuring that all parties have an opportunity to express their concerns, and guiding them towards finding common ground. By remaining impartial and objective, psychologists can help de-escalate conflicts and promote understanding and cooperation.

10.2.5 Conflict Management Training

Psychologists can also provide conflict management training to employees and leaders within an organization. This training equips individuals with the necessary skills and knowledge to identify, address, and resolve conflicts effectively. It may include workshops, role-playing exercises, and case studies to simulate real-life conflict scenarios. By empowering employees with conflict resolution skills, psychologists can create a culture of proactivity and self-sufficiency, where conflicts are addressed at an early stage before they escalate.

10.2.6 Emotional Intelligence and Empathy

Emotional intelligence and empathy play a crucial role in conflict resolution. Psychologists can help individuals develop emotional intelligence skills, such as self-awareness, self-regulation, empathy, and social skills. These skills enable individuals to understand their own emotions and the emotions of others, which can lead to more empathetic and compassionate conflict resolution. By fostering emotional intelligence within the organization, psychologists can create an environment where conflicts are approached with understanding and empathy.

To prevent conflicts from arising in the first place, psychologists can assist organizations in establishing clear policies and procedures. By defining expectations, roles, and responsibilities, organizations can minimize misunderstandings and potential sources of conflict. Psychologists can work with leaders and HR departments to develop comprehensive conflict resolution policies that outline the steps to be taken when conflicts arise. These policies can provide a framework for addressing conflicts in a fair and consistent manner.

10.2.8 Continuous Evaluation and Improvement

Conflict resolution strategies should not be seen as a one-time fix but rather as an ongoing process. Psychologists can help organizations establish mechanisms for continuous evaluation and improvement of conflict resolution practices. This may involve collecting feedback from employees, conducting regular assessments of conflict resolution effectiveness, and making necessary adjustments to the strategies and policies in place. By continuously evaluating and improving conflict resolution practices, psychologists can contribute to the creation of a healthier and more harmonious work environment.

In conclusion, the role of a psychologist in conflict resolution is vital for creating a positive and productive work environment. By understanding the nature of conflicts, promoting effective communication, facilitating collaboration and compromise, providing mediation and facilitation, offering conflict management training, fostering emotional intelligence and empathy, establishing clear policies and procedures, and continuously evaluating and improving conflict resolution practices, psychologists can help organizations address conflicts in a constructive and proactive manner. Through their expertise, psychologists contribute to the overall well-being and success of both individuals and the organization as a whole.

Mediation and facilitation techniques play a crucial role in resolving conflicts and promoting positive communication within an organization. As a psychologist, it is essential to understand and utilize these techniques effectively to create an aware corporate culture that fosters well-being in the workplace.

10.3.1 Mediation: A Collaborative Approach to Conflict Resolution

Mediation is a process in which a neutral third party, the mediator, helps facilitate communication and negotiation between conflicting parties. The goal of mediation is to find a mutually acceptable solution that addresses the underlying issues and restores harmony in the workplace.

In the context of creating an aware corporate culture, psychologists can act as mediators to resolve conflicts between employees, teams, or even between employees and management. By employing active listening skills, empathy, and impartiality, psychologists can create a safe and supportive environment for open dialogue and problem-solving.

During the mediation process, the psychologist mediates discussions, encourages each party to express their concerns and perspectives, and helps them understand each other's viewpoints. The psychologist also assists in identifying common ground and exploring potential solutions that meet the needs of all parties involved.

Mediation not only resolves conflicts but also promotes understanding, empathy, and collaboration among employees. By facilitating effective communication and encouraging a cooperative mindset, psychologists can contribute to the development of an aware corporate culture that values open dialogue and respectful interactions.

Facilitation techniques are valuable tools for psychologists to enhance communication and collaboration within an organization. Facilitation involves guiding group discussions, brainstorming sessions, and decision-making processes to ensure active participation and effective outcomes.

In the context of creating an aware corporate culture, psychologists can use facilitation techniques to promote open communication, encourage diverse perspectives, and foster a sense of ownership and accountability among employees. By creating a structured and inclusive environment, psychologists can help teams work together more effectively and make informed decisions.

During facilitation sessions, psychologists employ various techniques such as active listening, summarizing key points, asking open-ended questions, and managing time effectively. These techniques help ensure that all voices are heard, ideas are explored, and conflicts are addressed constructively.

Psychologists also play a crucial role in managing power dynamics within groups during facilitation. They ensure that all participants have an equal opportunity to contribute and that dominant voices do not overshadow others. By creating a safe and inclusive space, psychologists can empower employees to express their thoughts and ideas freely, leading to increased engagement and collaboration.

Facilitation techniques not only improve communication and collaboration but also contribute to the development of an aware corporate culture. By encouraging active participation, valuing diverse perspectives, and fostering a sense of ownership, psychologists can help create an environment where employees feel heard, respected, and motivated to contribute their best.

To effectively mediate conflicts and facilitate discussions, psychologists need to possess specific skills and knowledge. Training and skill development are essential for psychologists to enhance their abilities in mediation and facilitation techniques.

Psychologists can undergo specialized training programs that focus on conflict resolution, mediation, and facilitation skills. These programs provide them with a theoretical understanding of conflict dynamics, communication strategies, and negotiation techniques. Additionally, they offer practical experience through role-plays, case studies, and real-life simulations.

By continuously updating their knowledge and skills, psychologists can stay abreast of the latest research and best practices in mediation and facilitation. They can also learn new techniques and approaches that can be applied in different organizational contexts.

Furthermore, psychologists can collaborate with other professionals, such as conflict resolution specialists or facilitators, to exchange knowledge and learn from their experiences. By networking and participating in professional development opportunities, psychologists can expand their expertise and enhance their effectiveness in creating an aware corporate culture.

To create an aware corporate culture, mediation and facilitation techniques should be integrated into various organizational processes. Psychologists can work closely with human resources departments, managers, and leaders to embed these techniques into conflict resolution procedures, team-building activities, and decision-making processes.

For conflict resolution, psychologists can develop mediation guidelines and protocols that outline the steps to be followed when conflicts arise. These guidelines can include the involvement of a psychologist as a neutral mediator, the process for scheduling and conducting mediation sessions, and the principles of confidentiality and impartiality.

In team-building activities, psychologists can facilitate discussions and exercises that promote open communication, trust-building, and collaboration. These activities can help team members understand each other's strengths, weaknesses, and communication styles, leading to improved teamwork and a more aware corporate culture.

In decision-making processes, psychologists can facilitate meetings and discussions to ensure that all relevant perspectives are considered. By employing facilitation techniques, psychologists can guide the group towards consensus and help prevent conflicts or biases from hindering the decision-making process.

By integrating mediation and facilitation techniques into organizational processes, psychologists can create a culture that values open communication, collaboration, and constructive conflict resolution. This, in turn, contributes to the overall well-being of employees and the organization as a whole.

Conclusion

Mediation and facilitation techniques are powerful tools that psychologists can utilize to create an aware corporate culture. By mediating conflicts, facilitating discussions, and integrating these techniques into organizational processes, psychologists can foster open communication, collaboration, and constructive conflict resolution. Through their role in mediation and facilitation, psychologists contribute to the development of a positive and supportive work environment that promotes employee well-being and organizational success.

10.4 Promoting Positive Conflict Resolution in the Organization

Conflict is an inevitable part of any organization. It can arise from differences in opinions, goals, or values among employees. However, if left unresolved, conflict can have a detrimental impact on employee well-being and overall organizational productivity. Therefore, it is crucial for organizations to promote positive conflict resolution strategies to create a harmonious work environment. In this section, we will explore the role of the psychologist in promoting positive conflict resolution in the organization.

10.4.1 Understanding the Nature of Conflict

Before delving into conflict resolution strategies, it is important to understand the nature of conflict. Conflict can be categorized into two types: constructive and destructive. Constructive conflict, also known as functional conflict, refers to disagreements that lead to positive outcomes such as increased creativity, innovation, and improved decision-making. On the other hand, destructive conflict, also known as dysfunctional conflict, is characterized by hostility, aggression, and negative emotions, which can have detrimental effects on individuals and the organization as a whole.

Psychologists play a crucial role in helping organizations identify and differentiate between constructive and destructive conflict. By understanding the underlying causes and dynamics of conflict, psychologists can develop effective strategies to promote positive conflict resolution.

10.4.2 Creating a Culture of Open Communication

One of the key factors in promoting positive conflict resolution is creating a culture of open communication within the organization. Psychologists can assist in fostering an environment where employees feel comfortable expressing their concerns, ideas, and opinions without fear of retribution. This can be achieved through various means, such as conducting workshops on effective communication, providing training on active listening skills, and encouraging regular feedback sessions.

By promoting open communication, psychologists can help employees address conflicts in a timely manner, preventing them from escalating into more serious issues. Additionally, open communication allows for the identification of underlying causes of conflict, enabling organizations to implement targeted interventions to address these issues.

10.4.3 Implementing Conflict Resolution Training

Psychologists can also play a vital role in implementing conflict resolution training programs within organizations. These programs aim to equip employees with the necessary skills and techniques to effectively manage and resolve conflicts. Conflict resolution training typically covers topics such as active listening, assertiveness, problem-solving, and negotiation skills.

Through conflict resolution training, employees can develop a better understanding of their own conflict management styles and learn how to adapt their approach to different situations. By providing employees with the tools and knowledge to handle conflicts constructively, psychologists can contribute to a more positive and productive work environment.

10.4.4 Mediation and Facilitation

In situations where conflicts have escalated and direct communication between parties is challenging, psychologists can act as mediators or facilitators. Mediation involves a neutral third party assisting conflicting parties in reaching a mutually acceptable resolution. Psychologists with expertise in conflict resolution can guide the mediation process, ensuring that all parties have an opportunity to express their concerns and work towards a mutually beneficial solution.

Facilitation, on the other hand, involves psychologists assisting in group discussions or meetings where conflicts may arise. By providing a neutral perspective and facilitating effective communication, psychologists can help parties involved in the conflict to find common ground and work towards a resolution.

Psychologists can also contribute to promoting positive conflict resolution by fostering a collaborative work environment. Collaboration encourages employees to work together towards shared goals, fostering a sense of unity and reducing the likelihood of conflicts arising. Psychologists can assist in creating collaborative structures and processes within the organization, such as cross-functional teams, project-based work, and shared decision-making.

By promoting collaboration, psychologists can help employees develop a better understanding and appreciation for each other's perspectives, reducing the potential for conflicts to arise. Additionally, a collaborative work environment encourages open dialogue and problem-solving, allowing conflicts to be addressed and resolved more effectively.

To ensure that conflicts are addressed consistently and fairly, psychologists can assist organizations in establishing conflict resolution policies and procedures. These policies outline the steps to be followed when conflicts arise, ensuring that all parties involved are aware of the process and their rights.

Psychologists can help organizations develop conflict resolution policies that are aligned with best practices and legal requirements. These policies may include guidelines on reporting conflicts, the involvement of mediators or facilitators, and the escalation process if conflicts cannot be resolved informally.

10.4.7 Monitoring and Evaluation

Lastly, psychologists can contribute to promoting positive conflict resolution by monitoring and evaluating the effectiveness of conflict resolution strategies within the organization. By collecting feedback from employees, conducting surveys, and analyzing conflict resolution outcomes, psychologists can identify areas for improvement and make necessary adjustments to the conflict resolution approach. Regular monitoring and evaluation allow organizations to assess the impact of conflict resolution strategies on employee well-being and organizational performance. Psychologists can provide valuable insights and recommendations based on the data collected, ensuring that conflict resolution efforts are continuously improved and aligned with the goals.

In conclusion, the role of the psychologist in promoting positive conflict resolution in the organization is crucial. By understanding the nature of conflict, creating a culture of open communication, implementing conflict resolution training, facilitating mediation and facilitation, promoting a collaborative work environment, establishing conflict resolution policies and procedures, and monitoring and evaluating conflict resolution efforts, psychologists can contribute to creating a harmonious and productive work environment.

CHAPTER XI

THE IMPORTANCE OF EMPLOYEE SUPPORT PROGRAMS

11.1 Types of Employee Support Programs

Employee support programs play a crucial role in creating a healthy and supportive work environment. These programs are designed to provide employees with the necessary resources and support to address various personal and professional challenges they may face. By offering a range of services and interventions, employee support programs aim to enhance well-being, promote work-life balance, and improve overall job satisfaction. In this section, we will explore the different types of employee support programs that organizations can implement to support their employees.

11.1.1 Employee Assistance Programs (EAPs)

Employee Assistance Programs (EAPs) are one of the most common types of employee support programs. EAPs are confidential counseling services that provide employees with professional assistance to address personal and work-related issues. These programs typically offer short-term counseling sessions, referrals to specialized services, and resources for managing various challenges such as stress, substance abuse, mental health issues, and financial difficulties. EAPs are designed to help employees overcome personal obstacles that may affect their well-being and job performance.

11.1.2 Wellness Programs

Wellness programs focus on promoting physical and mental well-being among employees. These programs often include initiatives such as fitness classes, health screenings, nutrition counseling, and stress management workshops. Wellness programs aim to educate employees about healthy lifestyle choices and provide them with the tools and resources to improve their overall well-being. By encouraging employees to prioritize their health, organizations can create a culture that values and supports employee well-being.

11.1.3 Work-Life Balance Programs

Work-life balance programs are designed to help employees manage their personal and professional responsibilities effectively. These programs recognize the importance of maintaining a healthy equilibrium between work and personal life. Work-life balance programs may include flexible work arrangements, such as telecommuting or flexible scheduling, as well as policies that support parental leave, caregiving, and time off for personal reasons. By providing employees with the flexibility to meet their personal obligations, organizations can reduce stress and enhance overall job satisfaction.

11.1.4 Mental Health Support Programs

Mental health support programs focus specifically on addressing the mental well-being of employees. These programs aim to reduce the stigma associated with mental health issues and provide employees with the necessary resources and support to manage their mental health effectively. Mental health support programs may include access to mental health professionals, counseling services, stress management workshops, and educational resources on mental health awareness. By prioritizing mental health, organizations can create a supportive environment that promotes psychological well-being.

11.1.5 Financial Wellness Programs

Financial wellness programs aim to support employees in managing their financial well-being. These programs provide resources and education on budgeting, saving, investing, and managing debt. Financial wellness programs may also offer access to financial advisors or workshops on financial planning. By addressing financial stress and promoting financial literacy, organizations can help employees improve their overall well-being and reduce distractions that may impact their job performance.

11.1.6 Career Development Programs

Career development programs focus on supporting employees in their professional growth and advancement. These programs may include mentoring initiatives, training and development opportunities, and career coaching. By investing in employees' professional development, organizations can enhance job satisfaction, increase employee engagement, and promote a positive work culture.

11.1.7 Diversity and Inclusion Programs

Diversity and inclusion programs aim to create an inclusive work environment that values and respects individuals from diverse backgrounds. These programs may include diversity training, employee resource groups, and initiatives to promote diversity in recruitment and hiring practices. By fostering a culture of inclusivity, organizations can enhance employee well-being and create a sense of belonging among employees.

11.1.8 Employee Recognition Programs

Employee recognition programs are designed to acknowledge and appreciate employees' contributions and achievements. These programs may include awards, incentives, and public recognition for outstanding performance. By recognizing and rewarding employees' efforts, organizations can boost morale, increase job satisfaction, and foster a positive work environment.

In conclusion, employee support programs are essential for creating a supportive and healthy work environment. By implementing a variety of programs that address different aspects of employee well-being, organizations can enhance job satisfaction, improve productivity, and promote a positive corporate culture. The role of the psychologist in employee support programs is to provide expertise in designing and implementing these programs, as well as offering counseling and support to employees who may require additional assistance. By working collaboratively with other professionals, psychologists can contribute to the development and success of employee support programs in organizations.

11.2 Implementing Employee Assistance Programs

Employee Assistance Programs (EAPs) are an essential component of creating a supportive and healthy work environment. These programs are designed to provide employees with the necessary resources and support to address personal and work-related challenges that may impact their well-being and performance. As a psychologist, your role in implementing EAPs is crucial in ensuring their effectiveness and promoting a culture of support within the organization.

11.2.1 Understanding the Purpose of Employee Assistance Programs

Before delving into the implementation process, it is important to understand the purpose and benefits of EAPs. These programs aim to assist employees in managing a wide range of personal and work-related issues, including stress, mental health concerns, substance abuse, financial difficulties, and relationship problems. By providing confidential and accessible support, EAPs can help employees navigate these challenges and improve their overall well-being.

11.2.2 Assessing the Organization's Needs

As a psychologist, your first step in implementing an EAP is to assess the specific needs of the organization. This involves conducting a thorough evaluation of the workplace culture, employee demographics, and existing support systems. By gathering data through surveys, interviews, and focus groups, you can gain valuable insights into the unique challenges faced by employees and identify areas where an EAP can make a significant impact.

11.2.3 Designing the Employee Assistance Program

Based on the needs assessment, you can then design an EAP that aligns with the organization's goals and values. This involves determining the scope of services to be offered, such as counseling, coaching, and referral services. Additionally, you will need to establish clear guidelines regarding confidentiality, accessibility, and the process for accessing EAP resources.

Collaborating with key stakeholders, such as human resources, management, and employee representatives, is crucial during the design phase. By involving these individuals, you can ensure that the EAP is tailored to meet the specific needs of the organization and gain their support for its implementation.

11.2.4 Establishing Partnerships with Service Providers

To effectively implement an EAP, it is essential to establish partnerships with external service providers. These providers may include mental health professionals, counselors, financial advisors, and legal experts, depending on the scope of services offered by the EAP. As a psychologist, you can play a vital role in selecting and vetting these providers to ensure their qualifications, expertise, and alignment with the organization's values.

By establishing strong partnerships, you can ensure that employees have access to high-quality and specialized support when needed. Regular communication and collaboration with service providers are also important to monitor the effectiveness of the EAP and make any necessary adjustments.

11.2.5 Promoting and Communicating the EAP

Implementing an EAP requires effective promotion and communication to ensure that employees are aware of its existence and understand how to access its services. As a psychologist, you can contribute to this process by developing communication strategies that effectively convey the benefits and purpose of the EAP.

Utilizing various communication channels, such as email, intranet, posters, and workshops, can help reach a wide range of employees. It is important to emphasize the confidentiality and non-judgmental nature of the EAP to encourage employees to seek support without fear of stigma or reprisal.

11.2.6 Training and Education

To maximize the impact of the EAP, it is crucial to provide training and education to both employees and managers. As a psychologist, you can develop and deliver workshops and training sessions that focus on topics such as stress management, mental health awareness, conflict resolution, and work-life balance.

By equipping employees and managers with the necessary knowledge and skills, you can empower them to proactively address challenges and utilize the resources provided by the EAP. Training sessions can also help reduce the stigma surrounding mental health and create a more supportive and understanding work environment.

11.2.7 Monitoring and Evaluation

Once the EAP is implemented, ongoing monitoring and evaluation are essential to ensure its effectiveness and make any necessary improvements. As a psychologist, you can contribute to this process by developing evaluation measures, such as surveys and feedback mechanisms, to gather data on employee satisfaction, utilization rates, and outcomes.

Regularly reviewing this data and analyzing trends can help identify areas of success and areas that may require further attention. By continuously monitoring and evaluating the EAP, you can ensure that it remains responsive to the changing needs of employees and the organization.

Implementing an EAP is not a one-time event but an ongoing process of continuous improvement. As a psychologist, you can play a vital role in driving this process by staying informed about the latest research and best practices in employee assistance programs.

By regularly reviewing and updating the EAP based on emerging trends and feedback from employees and stakeholders, you can ensure that it remains relevant, effective, and aligned with the organization's goals and values.

In conclusion, implementing an Employee Assistance Program requires careful planning, collaboration, and ongoing evaluation. As a psychologist, your role in this process is crucial in designing, promoting, and continuously improving the EAP to create a supportive and healthy work environment. By providing employees with the necessary resources and support, EAPs can contribute to their overall well-being and enhance the organization's productivity and success.

11.3 Mental Health Support in the Workplace

Mental health is a critical aspect of overall well-being, and it plays a significant role in the workplace. As organizations become more aware of the importance of mental health, they are recognizing the need for mental health support programs in the workplace. This is where psychologists can play a vital role in creating a supportive and mentally healthy work environment.

11.3.1 Understanding Mental Health in the Workplace

Before delving into the role of psychologists in mental health support programs, it is essential to understand the concept of mental health in the workplace. Mental health refers to a person's emotional, psychological, and social well-being. It affects how individuals think, feel, and act, and it also influences how they handle stress, relate to others, and make decisions.

In the workplace, mental health issues can have a significant impact on employees' well-being and productivity. Common mental health conditions such as anxiety, depression, and stress can lead to decreased job satisfaction, increased absenteeism, and reduced overall performance. Recognizing and addressing these issues is crucial for creating a positive work environment.

11.3.2 The Role of Psychologists in Mental Health Support Programs

Psychologists are uniquely qualified to contribute to mental health support programs in the workplace. With their expertise in human behavior, emotions, and mental processes, psychologists can provide valuable insights and interventions to promote mental well-being among employees. Here are some key roles psychologists can play in mental health support programs:

11.3.2.1 Assessing and Identifying Mental Health Needs

Psychologists can conduct assessments and evaluations to identify mental health needs within the organization. They can administer standardized tests, conduct interviews, and analyze data to gain a comprehensive understanding of the mental health challenges employees may be facing. By identifying these needs, psychologists can develop targeted interventions and support strategies.

11.3.2.2 Providing Individual Counseling and Therapy

One of the primary roles of psychologists in mental health support programs is to provide individual counseling and therapy to employees. They can offer a safe and confidential space for employees to discuss their mental health concerns, explore their emotions, and develop coping strategies. Through evidence-based therapeutic techniques, psychologists can help individuals manage stress, improve their mental well-being, and enhance their overall functioning.

11.3.2.3 Conducting Group Interventions and Workshops

Psychologists can also facilitate group interventions and workshops to address common mental health issues in the workplace. These interventions can focus on stress management, resilience building, mindfulness, and other relevant topics. By bringing employees together in a supportive group setting, psychologists can foster a sense of community, provide education on mental health, and teach practical skills for maintaining well-being.

11.3.2.4 Training and Education for Managers and Leaders

Psychologists can play a crucial role in training managers and leaders on how to support employees' mental health effectively. They can provide education on recognizing signs of mental distress, promoting a mentally healthy work environment, and responding appropriately to employee concerns. By equipping managers with the necessary knowledge and skills, psychologists can create a culture of support and understanding throughout the organization.

11.3.2.5 Developing Mental Health Policies and Programs

Psychologists can collaborate with human resources departments and organizational leaders to develop comprehensive mental health policies and programs. They can contribute their expertise in designing initiatives that promote mental well-being, such as employee assistance programs, stress reduction programs, and work-life balance initiatives. Psychologists can also provide guidance on implementing and evaluating these programs to ensure their effectiveness.

11.3.2.6 Crisis Intervention and Critical Incident Support

In times of crisis or critical incidents, psychologists can provide immediate support and intervention. They can help employees cope with traumatic events, manage their emotions, and facilitate the healing process. Psychologists can also assist in developing crisis response plans and protocols to ensure the organization is prepared to handle such situations effectively.

11.3.3 The Benefits of Mental Health Support Programs

Implementing mental health support programs in the workplace can have numerous benefits for both employees and the organization as a whole. Some of the key benefits include:

- Improved employee well-being and mental health
- Increased job satisfaction and engagement
- Reduced absenteeism and presenteeism
- Enhanced productivity and performance
- Decreased workplace conflicts and stress levels
- Improved retention and recruitment of talented employees
- Positive impact on the organization's reputation and brand image

By investing in mental health support programs and leveraging the expertise of psychologists, organizations can create a culture that prioritizes employee well-being and fosters a mentally healthy work environment.

Conclusion

Mental health support programs are essential for creating a supportive and mentally healthy workplace. Psychologists play a crucial role in designing, implementing, and evaluating these programs. By providing individual counseling, conducting group interventions, training managers, and developing policies, psychologists can contribute to the overall well-being of employees and the success of the organization. Prioritizing mental health in the workplace not only benefits employees but also leads to increased productivity, improved job satisfaction, and a positive organizational culture.

11.4 The Role of the Psychologist in Employee Support Programs

Employee support programs play a crucial role in promoting well-being in the workplace. These programs aim to provide employees with the necessary support and resources to address various personal and professional challenges they may face. As part of these programs, psychologists have a unique and important role to play in ensuring the success and effectiveness of such initiatives.

11.4.1 Understanding the Importance of Employee Support Programs

Employee support programs encompass a wide range of initiatives designed to support employees in various aspects of their lives. These programs can include mental health support, counseling services, wellness programs, work-life balance initiatives, and more. The goal of these programs is to create a supportive and inclusive work environment that promotes the well-being and productivity of employees.

Psychologists bring a wealth of knowledge and expertise to employee support programs. They have a deep understanding of human behavior, mental health, and the factors that contribute to overall well-being. By leveraging their expertise, psychologists can help organizations develop and implement effective support programs that address the unique needs of their employees.

11.4.2 Designing and Implementing Employee Support Programs

Psychologists play a crucial role in the design and implementation of employee support programs. They can collaborate with organizational leaders, human resources professionals, and other stakeholders to develop programs that align with the organization's goals and values. Psychologists can conduct needs assessments and gather data to identify the specific challenges and needs of employees, ensuring that the support programs are tailored to address these issues effectively.

Furthermore, psychologists can provide valuable insights into the most appropriate and evidence-based interventions and strategies to incorporate into these programs. They can draw from their knowledge of various therapeutic approaches, counseling techniques, and mental health interventions to design programs that are both effective and sustainable.

11.4.3 Providing Counseling and Mental Health Support

One of the key roles of psychologists in employee support programs is to provide counseling and mental health support to employees. Psychologists can offer individual counseling sessions to employees who may be experiencing personal or work-related challenges that impact their well-being. These sessions provide a safe and confidential space for employees to discuss their concerns, explore coping strategies, and develop resilience.

Psychologists can also facilitate group therapy sessions or support groups to address common challenges faced by employees. These sessions can focus on topics such as stress management, work-life balance, communication skills, and conflict resolution. By providing a supportive environment for employees to share their experiences and learn from one another, psychologists can foster a sense of community and connection within the organization.

11.4.4 Training and Education

In addition to providing direct counseling and support, psychologists can also play a vital role in training and educating employees and leaders on various aspects of well-being. They can deliver workshops and seminars on topics such as stress management, emotional intelligence, resilience, and work-life balance. These educational sessions can equip employees with the necessary skills and knowledge to navigate challenges effectively and promote their own well-being.

Psychologists can also provide training to managers and leaders on how to support their employees' well-being. This can include training on effective communication, conflict resolution, and creating a positive work environment. By empowering leaders with the tools and knowledge to support their teams, psychologists contribute to the overall well-being of the organization.

11.4.5 Evaluating and Improving Employee Support Programs

Another important role of psychologists in employee support programs is to evaluate their effectiveness and make necessary improvements. Psychologists can design and implement evaluation measures to assess the impact of these programs on employee well-being and organizational outcomes. They can collect and analyze data to determine the effectiveness of different interventions and identify areas for improvement.

Based on the evaluation findings, psychologists can collaborate with organizational leaders to make data-driven decisions and implement changes to enhance the effectiveness of employee support programs. This continuous improvement process ensures that the programs remain relevant and responsive to the evolving needs of employees.

11.4.6 Advocacy and Policy Development

Psychologists can also play a crucial role in advocating for employee well-being and influencing policy development within organizations. They can provide expert advice and guidance to organizational leaders on the importance of prioritizing employee support programs and creating a positive work environment. By advocating for the integration of well-being initiatives into organizational policies and practices, psychologists can contribute to the long-term well-being and success of employees.

In conclusion, psychologists have a vital role to play in employee support programs. Their expertise in understanding human behavior, mental health, and well-being allows them to design and implement effective programs that address the unique needs of employees. By providing counseling and mental health support, delivering training and education, evaluating program effectiveness, and advocating for employee well-being, psychologists contribute to creating a supportive and inclusive work environment that promotes the overall well-being of employees.

CHAPTER XII

MEASURING AND EVALUATING WELL-BEING IN THE WORKPLACE

12.1 Measuring Employee Well-being

Measuring employee well-being is a crucial step in creating a healthy and productive workplace. As a psychologist, it is essential to have reliable methods and tools to assess the well-being of employees accurately. By understanding the factors that contribute to employee well-being, organizations can identify areas for improvement and implement targeted strategies to enhance the overall work environment.

12.1.1 The Importance of Measuring Employee Well-being

Measuring employee well-being provides valuable insights into the overall health and satisfaction of the workforce. It allows organizations to identify potential issues and areas of improvement, leading to the development of effective interventions and initiatives. By regularly assessing employee well-being, organizations can track progress over time and evaluate the impact of their well-being strategies.

Furthermore, measuring employee well-being helps organizations understand the specific factors that influence employee satisfaction, engagement, and productivity. It enables them to identify the root causes of any problems and tailor interventions to address those issues directly. By focusing on employee well-being, organizations can create a positive work environment that fosters growth, productivity, and overall job satisfaction.

12.1.2 Methods for Measuring Employee Well-being

There are various methods and tools available to measure employee well-being. It is essential to select the most appropriate ones based on the organization's goals, resources, and the specific aspects of well-being to be assessed. Here are some commonly used methods:

Surveys and questionnaires are widely used to gather information about employee well-being. These tools typically include a series of questions that assess different dimensions of well-being, such as job satisfaction, work-life balance, stress levels, and overall happiness. Surveys can be administered online or in paper format, and the responses can be analyzed quantitatively to identify trends and patterns.

12.1.2.2 Focus Groups and Interviews

Focus groups and interviews provide an opportunity for employees to express their thoughts and feelings about their well-being in a more in-depth and qualitative manner. These methods allow for a deeper understanding of the factors that contribute to employee well-being and can uncover valuable insights that may not be captured through surveys alone. By engaging in open and honest conversations, psychologists can gain a more comprehensive understanding of the employees' experiences and perspectives.

12.1.2.3 Observations and Behavioral Assessments

Observations and behavioral assessments involve directly observing employees' behaviors and interactions in the workplace. This method can provide valuable information about the work environment, team dynamics, and individual well-being indicators. Psychologists can observe factors such as communication patterns, collaboration, and stress levels to gain insights into the overall well-being of employees.

12.1.2.4 Biometric Measures

Biometric measures, such as heart rate variability, cortisol levels, and sleep patterns, can provide objective data on employee well-being. These measures can help identify physiological indicators of stress, fatigue, and overall health. By combining biometric data with self-reported measures, psychologists can gain a more comprehensive understanding of employee well-being and its impact on performance.

12.1.3 Analyzing and Interpreting Employee Well-being Data

Once the data on employee well-being is collected, it is crucial to analyze and interpret the findings effectively. Psychologists can use statistical analysis techniques to identify patterns, correlations, and trends in the data. By comparing the results to benchmarks or previous assessments, psychologists can determine the effectiveness of well-being initiatives and identify areas for improvement.

It is essential to consider both individual and organizational factors when interpreting employee well-being data. Individual factors may include demographics, job roles, and personal circumstances, while organizational factors may include leadership styles, communication practices, and work environment. By considering these factors, psychologists can provide meaningful insights and recommendations to enhance employee well-being.

12.1.4 Using Employee Well-being Data to Drive Strategies

The data collected on employee well-being can serve as a valuable tool for organizations to develop and refine their well-being strategies. By identifying areas of concern and understanding the specific needs of employees, organizations can implement targeted interventions to address those issues effectively.

Psychologists play a crucial role in translating the data into actionable strategies. They can collaborate with organizational leaders, HR departments, and other stakeholders to develop evidence-based interventions that promote employee well-being. By leveraging their expertise in psychology and organizational behavior, psychologists can help organizations create a positive and supportive work environment that fosters employee well-being and overall organizational success.

In conclusion, measuring employee well-being is a vital step in creating a healthy and productive workplace. Psychologists play a crucial role in developing and implementing effective methods for assessing employee well-being. By analyzing and interpreting the data, psychologists can provide valuable insights and recommendations to enhance employee well-being. By using employee well-being data to drive strategies, organizations can create a positive work environment that promotes growth, productivity, and overall job satisfaction.

12.2 Assessing the Effectiveness of Well-being Initiatives

Assessing the effectiveness of well-being initiatives is crucial for organizations to understand the impact of their efforts on employee well-being and to make informed decisions about future strategies. As a psychologist, you play a vital role in this process by utilizing various assessment methods and tools to measure the effectiveness of well-being initiatives in the workplace.

12.2.1 The Importance of Assessment

Assessment is essential in determining whether well-being initiatives are achieving their intended goals and making a positive impact on employee well-being. It allows organizations to identify areas of success and areas that require improvement, enabling them to refine their strategies and allocate resources effectively. By assessing the effectiveness of well-being initiatives, organizations can ensure that their efforts are aligned with the needs and preferences of their employees, ultimately creating a healthier and more productive work environment.

12.2.2 Selecting Assessment Methods

When assessing the effectiveness of well-being initiatives, it is important to select appropriate assessment methods that align with the goals and objectives of the initiatives. There are various methods available, including surveys, interviews, focus groups, and observation. Each method has its strengths and limitations, and as a psychologist, you can help organizations choose the most suitable methods based on their specific needs and resources.

Surveys are commonly used to gather quantitative data and measure employee perceptions and experiences. They can be designed to assess specific aspects of well-being, such as work-life balance, stress levels, job satisfaction, and engagement. Surveys can provide valuable insights into the overall impact of well-being initiatives and identify areas that require further attention.

Interviews and focus groups, on the other hand, allow for more in-depth exploration of employee experiences and perceptions. These methods provide qualitative data and can uncover valuable insights that may not be captured through surveys alone. By conducting interviews or facilitating focus groups, you can gain a deeper understanding of the impact of well-being initiatives on individual employees and identify specific challenges or successes.

Observation is another valuable assessment method that involves directly observing workplace dynamics and employee behaviors. By observing interactions, work processes, and the overall atmosphere, you can assess the extent to which well-being initiatives have influenced the workplace culture and employee well-being. Observation can provide valuable contextual information and help identify any discrepancies between stated policies and actual practices.

12.2.3 Analyzing and Interpreting Data

Once the data has been collected through the chosen assessment methods, the next step is to analyze and interpret the findings. As a psychologist, you have the expertise to analyze both quantitative and qualitative data and draw meaningful conclusions from the results.

Quantitative data, such as survey responses, can be analyzed using statistical techniques to identify patterns, trends, and correlations. This analysis can provide organizations with valuable insights into the overall impact of well-being initiatives and help identify specific areas that require attention or improvement.

Qualitative data, obtained through interviews, focus groups, or observation, requires a different approach to analysis. It involves identifying themes, patterns, and commonalities in the data to gain a deeper understanding of employee experiences and perceptions. Qualitative analysis can provide rich insights into the subjective experiences of employees and help organizations understand the underlying factors influencing well-being.

12.2.4 Reporting and Feedback

After analyzing the data, it is essential to communicate the findings effectively to key stakeholders within the organization. As a psychologist, you can prepare comprehensive reports that summarize the assessment results, highlight key findings, and provide recommendations for further action.

The reports should be tailored to the specific audience, ensuring that the information is presented in a clear and accessible manner. Visual aids, such as charts or graphs, can be used to enhance understanding and facilitate decision-making. Additionally, you can provide verbal feedback and engage in discussions with organizational leaders to ensure a thorough understanding of the assessment findings and their implications.

Assessment is not a one-time process but rather an ongoing endeavor. Organizations should use the assessment results to drive continuous improvement in their well-being initiatives. By identifying areas that require attention or improvement, organizations can develop targeted strategies to address these issues and enhance employee well-being.

As a psychologist, you can collaborate with organizational leaders to develop action plans based on the assessment findings. These action plans may involve refining existing initiatives, introducing new programs, or implementing specific interventions to address identified challenges. By continuously monitoring and reassessing the effectiveness of these initiatives, organizations can ensure that they are making progress towards creating a healthier and more supportive work environment.

Conclusion

Assessing the effectiveness of well-being initiatives is a critical step in creating a positive and supportive work environment. As a psychologist, your role in this process is invaluable. By selecting appropriate assessment methods, analyzing and interpreting data, and providing feedback and recommendations, you can help organizations make informed decisions and drive continuous improvement in their well-being initiatives. Through your expertise, organizations can create a workplace culture that prioritizes employee well-being and fosters a sense of fulfillment and engagement among employees.

12.3 Using Data to Drive Well-being Strategies

In order to create a well-being focused workplace, it is essential to have a data-driven approach. Data provides valuable insights into the current state of well-being within an organization and helps identify areas that need improvement. By using data to drive well-being strategies, psychologists can effectively measure the impact of interventions and make informed decisions to enhance employee well-being.

12.3.1 Collecting Data on Employee Well-being

To begin using data to drive well-being strategies, it is important to collect relevant data on employee well-being. This can be done through various methods such as surveys, interviews, focus groups, and observation. Surveys are a commonly used tool to gather quantitative data on employee well-being. They can be designed to assess various aspects of well-being, including physical health, mental health, work-life balance, job satisfaction, and stress levels.

In addition to surveys, qualitative methods such as interviews and focus groups can provide valuable insights into the experiences and perceptions of employees regarding well-being in the workplace. These methods allow employees to share their thoughts, concerns, and suggestions, providing a deeper understanding of the factors that influence well-being.

Psychologists can also utilize observation techniques to gather data on employee well-being. By observing workplace dynamics, interactions, and behaviors, psychologists can gain valuable insights into the overall well-being climate within the organization.

12.3.2 Analyzing and Interpreting Data

Once the data on employee well-being is collected, it needs to be analyzed and interpreted to identify patterns, trends, and areas of concern. Psychologists can use statistical analysis techniques to examine the data and draw meaningful conclusions. This analysis can help identify specific areas where well-being is lacking or where interventions are needed.

By examining the data, psychologists can identify key factors that contribute to employee well-being, such as workload, work-life balance, job satisfaction, and interpersonal relationships. They can also identify potential stressors and risk factors that may negatively impact well-being.

12.3.3 Identifying Well-being Strategies

Using the insights gained from data analysis, psychologists can develop targeted well-being strategies to address the identified areas of concern. These strategies can be tailored to the specific needs and challenges of the organization.

For example, if the data reveals high levels of stress among employees, psychologists can develop stress management programs that provide employees with tools and techniques to cope with stress effectively. These programs may include stress reduction workshops, mindfulness training, and relaxation techniques.

If work-life balance is identified as an issue, psychologists can work with the organization to implement policies and practices that promote work-life balance, such as flexible work schedules, remote work options, and family-friendly policies.

12.3.4 Implementing and Evaluating Well-being Initiatives

Once the well-being strategies are developed, psychologists play a crucial role in implementing and evaluating these initiatives. They can collaborate with organizational leaders, human resources, and other stakeholders to ensure the successful implementation of the strategies.

Psychologists can also monitor and evaluate the effectiveness of the well-being initiatives by collecting additional data and feedback from employees. This ongoing evaluation allows for adjustments and improvements to be made to the strategies as needed.

12.3.5 Using Technology for Data-Driven Well-being Strategies

Advancements in technology have made it easier to collect and analyze data on employee well-being. Psychologists can leverage technology tools such as well-being apps, wearable devices, and online surveys to gather real-time data on employee well-being.

These technological tools can provide continuous monitoring of well-being indicators, allowing psychologists to identify trends and patterns more efficiently. They can also provide personalized feedback and recommendations to employees based on their individual well-being data.

12.3.6 Ethical Considerations in Data Collection and Analysis

When using data to drive well-being strategies, psychologists must adhere to ethical guidelines and ensure the privacy and confidentiality of employee data. It is important to obtain informed consent from employees before collecting any personal data and to use secure methods for data storage and analysis.

Psychologists should also consider the potential biases and limitations of the data collected. It is essential to interpret the data in a holistic manner, taking into account the complex nature of well-being and the various factors that influence it.

12.3.7 Collaboration with Stakeholders

To effectively use data to drive well-being strategies, psychologists need to collaborate with various stakeholders within the organization. This includes leaders, managers, human resources, and employees themselves. By involving all relevant parties, psychologists can gain a comprehensive understanding of the organization's well-being needs and ensure that the strategies implemented are aligned with the overall goals and values of the organization.

Collaboration also fosters a sense of ownership and commitment among employees, increasing the likelihood of successful implementation and sustained improvements in well-being.

Using data to drive well-being strategies is an ongoing process. Psychologists should continuously monitor and evaluate the effectiveness of the strategies and make necessary adjustments based on the data collected. Well-being needs and challenges may evolve over time, and it is important to adapt the strategies accordingly.

By continuously improving and adapting well-being strategies based on data, psychologists can create a workplace culture that prioritizes employee well-being and fosters a positive and supportive environment.

In conclusion, using data to drive well-being strategies is essential for creating a well-being focused workplace. Psychologists play a crucial role in collecting, analyzing, and interpreting data on employee well-being. By identifying areas of concern and developing targeted strategies, psychologists can effectively enhance employee well-being. Collaboration with stakeholders and continuous evaluation and adaptation are key to ensuring the success of these strategies.

12.4 Continuous Improvement in Workplace Well-being

Continuous improvement is a crucial aspect of creating and maintaining a healthy and supportive work environment. In order to promote well-being in the workplace, it is essential for organizations to constantly assess and evaluate their strategies and initiatives. This is where the role of the psychologist becomes invaluable. Psychologists can play a significant role in facilitating continuous improvement in workplace well-being by providing expertise in data analysis, program evaluation, and feedback mechanisms.

12.4.1 Data Collection and Analysis

One of the first steps in continuous improvement is collecting and analyzing data related to employee well-being. Psychologists can assist organizations in developing comprehensive surveys, questionnaires, and other assessment tools to gather relevant data. These tools can be designed to measure various aspects of well-being, such as job satisfaction, work-life balance, stress levels, and overall mental health.

Psychologists can also help organizations analyze the collected data to identify trends, patterns, and areas of improvement. By utilizing statistical techniques and data visualization methods, psychologists can provide valuable insights into the current state of well-being in the workplace. This data-driven approach allows organizations to make informed decisions and prioritize areas that require attention.

12.4.2 Program Evaluation

Once data has been collected and analyzed, psychologists can assist in evaluating the effectiveness of existing well-being initiatives and programs. This involves assessing whether these initiatives are achieving their intended goals and making a positive impact on employee well-being. Psychologists can employ various evaluation methods, such as surveys, focus groups, and interviews, to gather feedback from employees and stakeholders.

By conducting program evaluations, psychologists can identify strengths and weaknesses in current initiatives. They can determine which programs are successful and should be continued, as well as identify areas that need improvement or require new interventions. This evaluation process helps organizations refine their strategies and ensure that resources are allocated effectively to support employee well-being.

12.4.3 Feedback Mechanisms

Psychologists can also play a crucial role in establishing feedback mechanisms within the organization. These mechanisms allow employees to provide input, suggestions, and concerns regarding well-being initiatives. Psychologists can design and implement anonymous feedback systems, such as suggestion boxes or online surveys, to encourage open and honest communication.

By actively seeking feedback from employees, organizations can gain valuable insights into their experiences and perceptions of well-being initiatives. Psychologists can then analyze this feedback and provide recommendations for improvement. This feedback loop ensures that the organization remains responsive to the evolving needs and expectations of its employees, fostering a culture of continuous improvement.

12.4.4 Collaboration and Training

In addition to data analysis, program evaluation, and feedback mechanisms, psychologists can also collaborate with other professionals within the organization to develop and deliver training programs. These programs can focus on topics such as stress management, resilience building, and promoting work-life balance. By providing employees with the necessary knowledge and skills, organizations can empower them to take an active role in their own well-being.

Psychologists can work closely with human resources departments and leadership teams to design and implement training programs that address specific needs identified through data analysis and feedback mechanisms. These programs can be delivered through workshops, seminars, or online platforms, ensuring accessibility for all employees.

Ultimately, the role of the psychologist in continuous improvement in workplace well-being is to help organizations create a culture that prioritizes and supports employee well-being. By utilizing data, evaluating programs, establishing feedback mechanisms, and providing training, psychologists can contribute to the ongoing efforts of organizations to enhance well-being in the workplace.

Psychologists can also serve as advocates for well-being, promoting awareness and understanding of the importance of employee well-being among leadership and employees alike. By actively engaging with stakeholders and fostering a collaborative approach, psychologists can help create an environment where well-being is valued, and continuous improvement is embraced as a shared responsibility.

In conclusion, the role of the psychologist in continuous improvement in workplace well-being is multifaceted. From data collection and analysis to program evaluation, feedback mechanisms, collaboration, and training, psychologists bring valuable expertise and insights to the table. By working together with organizations, psychologists can contribute to the creation of a supportive and thriving work environment that prioritizes the well-being of its employees.

AFTERWORD

As we conclude this exploration into the vital nexus of psychology and corporate culture, I am compelled to reflect on the transformative journey we have undertaken. "The Psychologist's Role in Creating Workplace Wellbeing" has been more than a guide; it has been a narrative of empowerment, a testament to the pivotal role psychologists play in sculpting the very essence of organizational success.

In our quest to understand and harness the intricacies of corporate culture, we have uncovered layers of significance—values that serve as the foundation, beliefs that shape the narrative, and a vision that propels organizations toward greatness. As we stand at the crossroads of theory and practice, it is abundantly clear that the psychologist's influence extends far beyond the confines of traditional therapeutic settings. We are architects of culture, weaving the fabric that not only defines an organization but molds its destiny.

This afterword is not just a conclusion; it is an invitation to carry forward the torch of enlightenment into the corridors of boardrooms and office spaces. The strategies and interventions we've explored are not merely theoretical constructs; they are the building blocks of workplaces where well-being thrives, where employees are not just contributors but active participants in a shared vision.

In the relentless pursuit of success, we must not lose sight of the human element—the beating heart within the corporate machinery. It is the duty of psychologists, leaders, and every individual vested in the prosperity of an organization to ensure that the pulse of well-being remains strong. From psychological safety nets to fostering emotional intelligence, from promoting work-life balance to resolving conflicts with empathy—these are not mere initiatives; they are the soul-stirring symphony that harmonizes success with the flourishing of the human spirit.

As we part ways, let us carry forth the wisdom gleaned from these pages into our professional landscapes. The psychologist's role is not confined to the pages of this book; it is an ongoing narrative, an evolving story shaped by each interaction, each decision, and each commitment to the well-being of those we serve.

May this afterword be a call to action—a call to champion workplace cultures that not only breed success but cultivate a profound sense of fulfillment. Let our endeavors be the ripples that create waves of positive change, transforming workplaces into sanctuaries of growth, resilience, and, above all, well-being.

In the ceaseless evolution of organizational dynamics, let us be the architects of cultures that stand the test of time—a legacy where success is measured not only in profits but in the enduring well-being of the individuals who collectively propel an organization toward greatness.

Immensely grateful

Robert Jhonson

Summary